How to File a UK Patent Yourself

The straight forward guide to filing a UK patent. Also includes how to register designs, register trademarks, copyright advice, how to profit from your ideas and much more.

Neil Ward

How To File A UK Patent Yourself

Text Copyright ©2016 Neil Ward

All Rights Reserved

No reproduction without permission

The author does not accept liabilities resulting from use of this information.

All feedback welcomed,

neil@fileaukpatent.co.uk

www.fileaukpatent.co.uk

PREFACE

This book has been written to assist anyone in taking legal ownership of rights to their ideas and inventions. Without any knowledge and experience, the world of patents, trademarks, registered designs and any other form of intellectual property can seem like a dark art, a source of confusion. Common belief is that to profit from your ideas you need patent protection and the only way to obtain this is to consult a legal professional. A legal professional, in the form of a patent attorney. Without this professional help, there is a great fear that someone will copy your idea for their own profit, at your expense. Most likely the copycat will be a large corporation with vast wealth and therefore greater legal resources than you. So the belief is that you must seek help from the professionals or get eaten alive. These legal professionals tend to be rather expensive to say the least. This seems rather unfair. Considering intellectual property is just an administration procedure to assign inventions and ideas to the rightful owner.

In an ideal world everyone would just be able to profit fairly from their ideas without any expensive lawyers (coughs and spits) getting involved. It does not have to be this way. You can get things underway yourself. You can file for a patent, registered a design or trademark etc. yourself. It really is not that difficult. You can get your projects underway without even setting foot in the patent attorney's office. And once more, it does not cost you too much either, just a little hard work.

Whatever your idea may be, this book will explain what protection is available to you, be it patents, registered designs, trademarks or copyright. With some knowledge of the available systems, you will be able to follow the simple instructions in this book that take you through all the necessary application processes. You will see that it is not always necessary to use a patent attorney. Using professionals will put off the vast majority of inventors and idea makers due to the high fees. It can typically cost £5,000 plus to file a simple patent this way. This is a huge risk to most and they may not even guarantee your application will get through the lengthy patent granting process. But there is an alternative.

This book will show you how to file your own patent. For a few hundred pounds, instead of a few thousand, you can have you patent filed and obtain patent pending protection. With a little knowledge, filing your own patent goes from a dark art to a simple formality. Follow this guide and you will be able to file your patent and open up a 1 year window to exploit your idea. 1 year after you file a patent, the process can start to get pricey. At the 1 year stage you will have to commence any international applications which commonly would involve a PCT (Patent Cooperation Treaty) application which will set you back around £2,500. Also at the 1 year mark you may decide to get a professional to reassess your patent, make changes and optimise your protection. The idea here is that within the first year you take your idea and do everything you can to make it a success. A year is enough time to develop your idea into a fully functioning product, produce prototypes, conduct testing, assess the market potential, gauge interest and pitch your idea to investors. Depending on your idea you may even be able to get the product to market within this year. With this in mind, within the first year of filing your patent yourself, you can easily gauge whether it is worth the money to take the application further. The cost of filing patents and other forms of intellectual property with professionals should not stop you progressing with your ideas. Get things started yourself by following the simple steps in this guide and discover the true potential of your ideas.

I tend to come up with many ideas. Most of them terrible, but a few of them have proved worthy of getting excited about. The first idea good enough to get excited about happened several years ago now. I came up with a simple idea and decided to test it. I next produced low cost prototype good enough to test whether the technology worked. I was blown away with how well it worked. I was excited and immediately looked into how to take things further.

Inexperience and a lack of knowledge meant my first thought was to find a patent attorney to patent my idea for me. Because that is what you do, right? A work colleague of mine had a contact who worked for a patent attorney, so I thought my luck was in and I would get 'mates rates'. I told him I had an idea that I wanted to get patent protection for it. He put me in touch with the attorney who provided me with some estimated costs for filing a patent. I couldn't believe how much they wanted. Just to file the initial UK application and associated initial stages, they were expecting it to cost around £4,500. On top of this, additional fees would be required should complications arise. At the time I was actually doing alright for myself and did have enough money in the bank. However I was saving money in order to purchase my first property and had no intention on handing over that sort of money. I also had no idea how I was going to cash in on my invention once the attorney worked his magic and placed a granted patent in my hand. I was still confident in the quality of my idea and decided to look into my options further. So I conducted my own research into what to do.

I did much research and read several books relating to help for inventors and intellectual property advice. I found that there is good advice out there on how to profit from your idea. There is a lot of advice on licensing, manufacturing and outsourcing. There is advice on intellectual property but I feel that there is a lack of information directly aimed at guidance on actually filing UK patent applications. Also there is a lack of guidance for filing other forms of intellectual property protection. Most of the advice out there simply states to seek the help of a professional patent attorney. I'm sure this is the best option should money be no object. A patent attorney will file a patent for your idea, whether it will make money or not. So there is still risk as professional help may be a bad investment. The majority of the advice out there stating "you must seek professional help" comes from books written by professional patent attorneys, so they would say that right? The IPO website has some good advice and guides including a patents application guide. However, although important to read, this guide is fairly brief and again advises that you seek professional help.

I also bought and read most guides aimed at people filing any sort of UK intellectual property. I found there is very little out there. For example, one book written by a legal expert is almost 900 pages in length and I reckon only 30 pages of this were anything to do with actually filing patents.

So this would be about 3% of the book. The rest was just large quantities of patent law case studies as the book is aimed at professionals enforcing patent law. The book was an extremely challenging read, and joking aside, I literally fell asleep several times whilst reading it. The book is a very powerful sedative indeed. I do not believe it has to be this way, and in this book I explain how a patent can be filed, in a simple to follow guide that does not require specialist legal knowledge. It is admittedly not the most gripping of subjects to write a book about, but I believe this guide does a great job of explaining what you need to know about intellectual property, how to file for it and suggestions on how to take your ideas forward.

I have tried to make this subject more interesting by injecting some of Britain's best loved things into this book in the form of tea, chocolate and humour. I did this in the obvious way by using a 'chocolate teapot' idea in the patent examples. Please bear with me on this as I believe the chocolate teapot example works well to explain what is required to file a patent for your idea, which I hope is not a chocolate tea pot. In fact, I think I have done such a good job that I am seriously considering filing patents for the chocolate teapot myself, the idea has grown on me.

I myself am a mechanical design engineer by trade. I design large commercial and industrial heating, cooling and ventilation systems. As a part of this I write engineering specifications which gave me the confidence to attempt to write a patent application myself without professional help. I believe after going through this process myself that anyone can do it. You don't have to be an engineer or have any technical qualifications. It really is not that difficult. This book is about me sharing a collection of knowledge gained by reading many books and personal experience in getting a patent application through the system. Looking back on my experience with filing my first patent I could save you years of time by passing on my knowledge. I want to share this with you as I believe there are no other such books out there. This may be stopping many good inventors and designers from acting on their ideas and taking the first steps towards creating a product by protecting their intellectual property. I also believe there are a massive number of great ideas not acted upon due to; lack of knowledge of the intellectual property systems in place; the cost of professional fees and the lack of knowledge of how to actually exploit ideas commercially. Knowledge of the intellectual property systems and how to use them paves the way to getting great ideas to market. Without such knowledge, the way forward is not clear and ideas go to waste. Do not let this happen to your idea. Get things under way. Remember, if you take the option of filing yourself, once things get going and you start making your fortunes, this is when you can pay the professionals to look over your intellectual property. If you have professionals look at your patent later, prior to one year after your initial filing date, they can always make changes to the patent, re-file it, or file further patents to protect your idea.

This book contains additional advice other than filing of patent applications and you may wish to skip to certain sections. If you have an idea and you are not sure of what intellectual property protection is right for you, or you are wondering how to develop your idea I recommend that you read this book from start to finish. Although patents and intellectual property may not be the most gripping of subjects, reading this book should not take you too long and you should gain some valuable knowledge. Below is a summary of the book's contents chapter by chapter;

Section One: Ground Work

Chapter 1- Patent Costs, summarises the various costs involved for the different options available to you.

Chapter 2- Getting Help, how to approach the experts and what to keep in mind when doing so.

Chapter 3- To patent or Not to Patent, find out if your idea actually qualifies for patent protection, how to search for prior art to make sure your ideas is new and look into what other forms of intellectual property are available for your idea.

Chapter 4- Patent Application Process and Time Scales discusses the various stages involved and how long to expect them to take.

Section Two: Writing Your Patent

Chapter 5- Writing Your Patent Description, the description section of your patent will include the title, background, statement of invention and advantages

Chapter 6- Producing Your Patent Drawings will go through the various options and some useful guidelines to adhere to.

Chapter 7- Writing Your Detailed Description will thrash out the technical details of your invention with reference to your drawings

Chapter 8- Writing Your Patent Claims, the crucial legal content of your patent application

Chapter 9- Writing Your Patent Abstract, this section appears at the start of your patent and summarises its content

Chapter 10 Formatting Your Application will go through how to present, format and submit your application

Section 3: After Your Initial Application

Chapter 11- Prototypes, Testing and Commercial Analysis, this is advice on bringing your idea to market.

Chapter 12- Request for Search, how to request the IPO to conduct a patent search and how to analyse the search results

Chapter 13- Other forms of Intellectual Property, how to register designs, register trademarks and a guide to copyright protection

Chapter 14- The Final Stages, a guide to the final stages of the patent application process and advice on international filing

There is also a website to accompany this book containing many links that you may find useful. The links include further information to assist your patent writing and recommended reads to assist you in exploiting your ideas. There are also contact details to send any feedback and further recommendations you may have so please pay a visit to www.fileaukpatent.co.uk.

Neil Ward, East Sussex, December 2016

CONTENTS

Preface   **3**

SECTION ONE: GROUNDWORK

1. PATENT COSTS   15

Professional costs
Self-filing
Summary of patent fees

2. GETTING HELP   21

Approaching others
Non-disclosure agreements
Finding professional help
Help from the intellectual property office

3. TO PATENT OR NOT TO PATENT   26

Patent requirements
Patent search
Other forms of intellectual property protection

4. PATENT APPLICATION PROCESS AND TIME SCALES   37

Patent process overview
Formal submission and preliminary examination
Patent search
Patent publication
Substantive examination
International applications
Summary of time lines and costs
Timing strategy

SECTION TWO: WRITING YOUR PATENT APPLICATION

CHAPTER 5 WRITING YOUR PATENT DESCRIPTION 47

Patent description
Title
Background
Statement of invention
Advantages

CHAPTER 6 PRODUCING YOUR PATENT DRAWINGS 53

Drawing method
Producing drawings by hand
Drawing examples

CHAPTER 7 WRITING YOUR DETAILED DESCRIPTION 63

Example detailed description

CHAPTER 8 WRITING YOUR PATENT CLAIMS 67

Claims format
Formulating your claims
Examples of claims

CHAPTER 9 WRITING YOUR ABSTRACT 71

Abstract example

CHAPTER 10 FORMATTING YOUR PATENT APPLICATION 73

Order of sections
Forms and payments

SECTION THREE: AFTER YOUR INITIAL APPLICATION

CHAPTER 11 PROTOTYPES, TESTING AND COMMERCIAL ANALYSIS — 77

Prototypes
Commercial assessments
Routes to market

CHAPTER 12 REQUEST FOR SEARCH — 85

Forms and costs
Search report
Next steps

CHAPTER 13 OTHER FORMS OF INTELLECTUAL PROPERTY — 91

Registered designs
Design right
Trademarks
Copyright

CHAPTER 14 THE FINAL STAGES — 101

Substantive examination
International Filing
PCT route
PCT international stage
PCT national stage

FINAL THOUGHTS — 107

SECTION ONE: GROUNDWORK

Chapter 1 Patent Costs

Professional Costs

When it comes to patenting your invention, the general consensus and advice out there is to seek the help of a professional chartered patent attorney to help file your application.

If you approach a patent attorney they will often give a free consultation session to assess your invention. It is very likely that they will react extremely positively to the idea and give you a lovely warm and glowing feeling inside. You will then receive a fee quotation for a large sum of money. In return, the attorney will file a patent application for your idea. It is likely that they will first charge you to conduct a detailed search to confirm your idea is original. If they do find something to suggest that your idea is not original, you would have just wasted a large amount of money paying someone an over inflated fee to do something you could have easily done yourself.

If they believe your invention is new they then will charge you more of your life savings to continue the patent application. Even if they do not find anything in their prior art search, there is no guarantee the UK intellectual property office (IPO) will not. They conduct their own search, after your application is filed. If the IPO do find anything then you have wasted even more money on the professionals. If they do manage to get your idea thorough the entire patent process there is no guarantee that a granted patent is going to make you any money. The point here is that even if you do decided to spend the money on a professional patent attorney to carry out your application, there really is no guarantee that your invention will generate any money. So you will be spending your precious saving at a risk.

The attorney fees are likely to be in excess of £5,000.00 and that is just for a straight forward simple idea. You may have paid a large sum of money for a white elephant as there is no guarantee anyone will be interested in licencing or purchasing your finished product.

After your initial free consultation you will probably be left feeling incredible proud of yourself for your ground breaking idea, as re-enforced up by your new best friend the attorney. But you will also be left with a big decision to make. Do you pay the £5,000 to realise your dream or do you shelve your precious creation? If you have bags of spare cash then the attorney's offer maybe your best choice. Bear in mind, to make your creation a product on the shop shelves there will be other costs too. There will be costs for prototypes, marketing, manufacturing etc. All of this needs to be analysed.

You may not have bags of money. Even if you could beg, steal and borrow enough wonga together to hand over, it may not be worth the risk. You may have the money but decide it is not worth spending the kid's inheritance, upset your partner or spending all your hard earnt beer tokens on something that has a high risk associated with it. However, there is another option. You could politely (or impolitely) decline the patent attorney's offer and get things moving yourself. You can get the whole patent process underway for next to nothing, you just require use of a computer with internet access or a couple of stamps. If you carry out the whole process yourself, from the initial filing to the granting of your patent, it could only cost you £250. If you are like me, you may decide that £250 is worth risking in order realise your invention's potential. All it takes is a little hard work (not too hard).

Many people come up with good ideas and are instantly put off taking things any further by the fees involved in filing a patent with an attorney. This is very understandable. At first, the idea can seem completely overwhelming and daunting. With a little knowledge of the system, how it works and the paperwork involved, I believe anyone is perfectly capable of filing their own patent application. If you have the Brain to invent something in the first place and the initiative to pick up this book, then you are more than capable of using the patent system to your advantage. It may be that you protect your invention/ idea with other forms of intellectual property (IP). This is no problem as we will run through the other forms of protection and how to utilise these to your advantage. We will find out which IP is right for your creation in chapter 3.

In an ideal world the patent system would reward those with the best ideas, not those with the most expensive and best patent attorneys. The system would be in place to protect those with good ideas not those with the best knowledge of the system. In an ideal world you would have just thought of your new idea and a big cheque would have floated out the air, into your lap, and the hand of god would have patted you on the back whilst saying 'good idea'. Unfortunately it is not quite as simple as that. However, and thankfully, there is a system in place and your idea can become a reality, protected from copy cats so only you can exploit it. We first require a little knowledge of how the patent system works in order to take advantage of it. Luckily for you that is where this book comes in handy.

SELF-FILING

Filing yourself has many advantages. The most obvious is the cost savings. It means that giving your idea a chance of success need not be a huge decision and financial gamble. You may have many ideas and can give them all a chance.

Filing with a patent attorney will still need you to invest some of your precious time, despite the costs. This is because you will need to sit down and explain to them exactly what your invention is in detail. No one will understand your idea quite as well as yourself so in theory you are the best person to file your application. One of the most important advantages in my opinion is the fact that you can feel a sense of achievement and satisfaction in getting it done yourself. You don't have to feel reliant on someone else in order to protect your idea. If you have further ideas it is best to know how to protect them yourself without having to consult the professionals every time.

SUMMARY OF PATENT FEES

Professional fees are typically £5,000 to £20,000 depending on the type of invention. It is likely that the initial patent drafting will cost between £2000 and £5000. After this you will have to pay for the attorney to follow up correspondence with the IPO and take the application through the other stages which is likely to cost a further £3000 to £15,000 overall.

Self-filing fees- £230 plus your time for research and administration. This is broken down as follows;

-Application fee £30 (£20 if done electronically)

-Request for search Fee £150 (£130 if done electronically), this has to be done within 1 year of the initial filing date

-Request for substantive examination £100 (£80 if filed electronically), this has to be done usually around 2 years after the initial filing date.

Once you have a granted patent, you will have to pay renewal fees. These are due annually and commence 3 months after your patent granting date. The fees start at £70 but increase annually up to £600. The patent can be renewed for up to 20 years. By the time you need to consider renewal fees you should already be profiting from your idea so it is probably not worth worrying about them until further down the line. By this, it should be an easy decision whether or not to renew your patent each year. In the next chapter we will delve into getting external help in greater detail.

Chapter 2 Getting Help

Approaching Others

So you need to speak to someone about your amazing invention or idea? This is likely to be before you have any intellectual property in place protecting your idea. Maybe you wish to talk to a professional patent attorney or an industry expert for a little help and advice? It could be that you wish to discuss your idea with a potential investor and gauge their level of interest before committing your much valued time and money. This could be someone you don't necessary know and therefore have no reason to trust. You could be a little uneasy about this and rightfully so. How do you know they will not steal your idea? Or possibly talk about your idea to someone else, who in turn, will attempt to exploit your idea for their own gain? Rest easy because there are a few things we can do to help prevent this from happening.

You can provide yourself with some level of comfort by first agreeing to a non-disclosure agreement prior to sharing your idea. A non-disclosure agreement (NDA) is a signed agreement (contract) between two parties; the person you are approaching and you. The NDA commits the person you discuss your idea with to keeping all shared information confidential. They are not to divulge any aspects of your idea to anyone else without first obtaining your consent. They may ask you after to share information with manufacturers, suppliers etc. in order to assess the commercial potential of your product. They are also not at liberty to exploit your idea themselves for personal gain without your involvement and consent. This will give you some evidence in your favour should you need to take legal action against anyone.

There is a template NDA available on the IPO website which is easy to use. You can find it on the IPO website by searching non-disclosure agreements. The document is titled "one-way non-disclosure agreement" and is available in multiple formats. It is highly recommended that you have one in place before discussing your idea with anyone, especially if you have yet to obtain any protection for your idea. An NDA should be in place when first approaching a patent attorney or anyone for advice. Even after you have intellectual property protection, you may wish to have a NDA in place before discussing your ideas as an extra layer of protection.

NON-DISCLOSURE AGREEMENTS

Filling in an NDA is straight forward. If you use the template provided by the IPO, you will be required to complete the following details;

- Name and addresses of who the agreement is between. If the person you are engaging is acting on behalf of a company (most likely) then it will be the company address required.

-The purpose of the NDA. This might be "to provide intellectual property advice and services".

-The length of time the agreement is for. If unsure, state this as "indefinitely".

-The form is to be signed under witness by both parties.

Any reputable company is likely to have no objections in completing their sections and will most likely insist that one is in place to protect themselves also. They may have their own company standard NDA that they wish to be used, which is fine, just make sure you are happy with the content and add any terms you think are missing. I wouldn't be too particular about the content of the NDA as this may put off any potential investors from talking to you in the first place. Best to treat it as a necessary evil to get out the way before the real communication can take place.

It can be a difficult should you require help to patent your product. Many inventors may be put off ever doing anything with their idea if they are reluctant to ask for help in protecting it through fear of copycats. They may lack the knowledge to file for intellectual property protection themselves. This means that a huge amount of good ideas could be going to waste. Not acting on your idea could mean later someone else comes up with the idea, or similar, profiting from it.

Do not let this happen to you. You deserve to benefit from your good idea. Seek advice from the professionals or continue reading and gain the knowledge to protect your idea yourself. Even if you do decide to consult an expert, I would still recommend reading the rest of this book as knowledge of the system, and the service you are paying for can only be of benefit to you. Besides, if you ask the experts for help they will still require you to give them the same information in order to file the patent application for you. Knowing what information the patent attorney will require from you will save time.

FINDING PROFESSIONAL HELP

To find a chartered patent attorney, you can visit the Chartered Institute of Patent Attorneys website www.cipa.org.uk. There you can search by location for a local member. Alternatively just google it, there are many out there. You should also be able to find reviews and recommendations posted on-line by third parties.

HELP FROM THE INTELLECTUAL PROPERTY OFFICE

Whether you reach out for any professional help or if you are going to file yourself, it is highly recommended that you read the available help and guidance provided online by the IPO. The IPO guidance and help is free to access and written by the very same people that run the system. In particular they have a downloadable guide that tells you how to file your patent application. This is a PDF file titled 'Patents: Applications Guide'. Although they suggest you should seek the help of a professional patent attorney, it does go through a patent application example and highlights the administrative requirements to be met. I strongly recommend that you read the guide, in addition to this book. The IPO guide is a little brief and this book aim to fill in the gaps to help you complete an application. This book will also let you in on a few things that the IPO do not tell you.

It is worth stressing the fact that the IPO are extremely helpful to independent inventors. I have been quite amazed by how helpful they have been every time I have contacted them to ask advice or chase my applications. The UK invests a lot of money into the IPO. This is because intellectual property is a great source of wealth for the country. The UK is historically a hot spot for inventors and creative people. It may be in the genes or a product of our education system, but for whatever reason we seem to have a special ability for invention, design and culture. It is Intellectual property laws that allow us to profit from exporting this talent around the globe and I believe it is for this reason that the IPO are so helpful. You should take advantage of this. They will help you and in turn, if your idea is a success, it helps the nation's economy. Be a part of our countries greatest export, the Great British brain.

The next chapter will explain what kind of ideas you can protect with intellectual property and takes you through the first steps to take whether or not you are planning on seeking professional help.

CHAPTER 3 TO PATENT OR NOT TO PATENT

PATENT REQUIREMENTS

Before you start writing a patent application, it is important to first establish that your idea meets the minimum legal criteria. To have a patent granted, the invention must meet the following basic requirements as set out in patent law;

- Ownership- You must own the idea
- The invention must be novel and involve an 'inventive step'
- Must be capable of industrial application
- Must not be obvious

These requirements are expanded on below;

OWNERSHIP

Do you own your idea? Is there anyone else who helped you create the idea? A patent is a form of property, so if someone thinks they have a stake in your idea, they are entitled to claim their piece of the pie. If you are filing for a patent as a partnership with someone it does make things slightly more complicated. You will have to state the name of each inventor on the patent application form (form 1). If someone has helped you or contributed in some way they may have certain rights to the idea. This means when the riches start rolling in there could be a few arguments over the origins of the idea. Keeping your ideas to yourself proves beneficial. Keep your idea confidential. Do not tell anyone prior to filing the patent application. It maybe that you tell someone about it and they add something or even imagine they have helped you in some way due to conversations you have had. This can cause problems and conflict over the ownership of an idea. Only talk to trusted close family, or professionals that have signed a non-disclosure agreement. There is also the obvious risk of talking to someone and them stealing the idea by filing it first. You may talk to someone and they contribute an improvement which may complicate things. So best not discuss your idea in the first place, not without an NDA in place at least. If you are not the inventor, and filing on behalf of someone else, you will have to complete an extra form, 'Form 7 statement of inventorship and right to grant of a patent'. You can find this form on the IPO website.

To further protect the ownership to your idea, it is recommended you start a notebook detailing every action you take regarding the idea. This notebook needs to be a bound book and ideally you should write using permanent ink. This notebook serves as evidence of when you came up with your idea and tracks dates and details of any improvements, further ideas, communications with third parties, meeting dates etc. To further enforce your notebooks credibility, get someone to sign and date each notebook entry. This should be someone other than family. This will serve as evidence that someone has verified the content was produced by you on the date stated. This notebook will serve as evidence should it be required and also it should be a helpful record for yourself. Dates of communications and meeting notes can come in very handy.

Check that your employer is not entitled to your invention. If you are in employment, it may be that your employer is entitled to the rights of any intellectual property that you file for. This is only likely if you job position involves some sort of research and development or creativity it may be worth checking your contract just in case.

NOVELTY AND INVENTIVE STEP

The next requirement is that your idea must be novel and involve an inventive step. This means that it must be new and not an obvious progression of an existing idea, as judged by someone defined as 'skilled in the art' of that specific area of expertise. To be new, the idea must not appear on any other patent ever filed. That includes all patents from all over the world, ones that were not even granted or even past expired patents. Also this includes any product that has ever been made available to any market worldwide, even if it was not protected by a patent or other intellectual property. To check for other patents and technology similar to your idea, you conduct what is known as a patent search. This is covered later in this chapter.

The inventive step rule can be considered very objective. The IPO define it as something that would not be obvious to someone who is skilled in the art. For example, if you were to try and patent a TV with handles on either side for easy transport, this may be considered an obvious step. Or if you were to invent a beer tankard with two handles instead of one, this would be considered obvious. However, it may be possible to protect both of these ideas with a registered design, as long as the design is original and unique. We will look further at registered designs at the end of this chapter and how to file for them in chapter 13.

INDUSTRIAL APPLICATION

Your idea must be capable of industrial application. This basically means that it must have some sort of practical use. Hopefully this should be a fairly easy requirement to tick off. I would like to think it unlikely you have seriously considered filing a patent for something completely useless. So drop that chocolate tea pot idea.

NOT BE OBVIOUS

This is another slightly objective requirement. Basically your idea must not be obvious to someone who is 'skilled in the art'. Therefore it must not be obvious to someone who is a professional in the industry your idea belongs. So if your idea is to just combine to existing items together, such as a hammer with a screwdriver as a handle, it is unlikely to get approval from the IPO. Your idea should meet this criterion, for if it were obvious, it is likely that it would already exist. You will find it when you conduct your search. As long as it has a use, i.e. industry application, if it was obvious it would likely be available already, or at least someone would have made it in the past, or filed a patent for a similar idea. Best not get too hung up on this 'not obvious' requirement just yet, but it will come into play later when we produce the patent application in section 2.

PATENT SEARCH

After you file a patent with the IPO, you must pay them to carry out a 'search'. The search is for any 'prior art' that is similar to your idea. So they search for other similar patents in the same field. Should they decide that your patent is too similar to any previously filed, they will provide you feedback with their objections. For more information on the IPO patent search step of the process, please see chapter 12. For now, before you consider filing your idea, it is best to carry out your own initial patent search. This could save a lot of time and money should the idea prove not original.

The first step in your initial search is an obvious one, google it. Use google or any internet search engine to attempt to find any other products similar to your idea. If anything is for sale or you find any images that look similar to your idea it may be difficult to acquire patent protection. When searching, make sure you don't just have a brief attempt at a few keywords and then decide the idea is new. Make sure you have a good search. This is in a way, counter intuitive to the progress of your idea as you are trying to disprove its worth, but you need to be brutal with yourself. Try as many key words as you can think of. Make sure that if your idea could be used in different applications that you search all of these. Make sure you are honest with yourself. If you do find something similar, be objective. Do you think a patent examiner will consider your idea novel? If not, best to cut your losses now. If you proceed with a patent application that you know will not be successful, you will waste a considerable amount of time and money.

If you do not find any evidence of your idea on the internet search engines, firstly well done. Secondly, you will need to move on to the next stage and conduct a preliminary patent search. It is fairly straight forward and easy to carry out so it would be strange to pay an attorney or the IPO to do this without at least first carrying out an initial search yourself. There are a few different websites that you can use to carry out a search. The most common to use is ESPACENET, https://worldwide.espacenet.com/ . This is the EPO's (European Patent Office) patent search resource. As with your standard internet search, make sure you try all key words you can think of. Have a look at the patents that come up and be very honest with yourself over whether they include your idea. Read the abstracts at the beginning of the patent documents to gauge whether or not it is worth reading the rest of the patent for similarities with your idea. I also recommend having a quick look at any drawings that come up. Even if the patent appears to be technically different, the patent drawings may appear to have some sort of resemblance to your idea. If this is the case, fear not, it will not necessarily stop you from getting a patent but you will have to reference this patent in your application and highlight the differences to the examiners.

So make sure you make a note of and preferable save a copy of any patents that have any vaguely similar drawings and content to your own idea. If you are struggling to find anything similar at all, you should still try and collect a few patents in a similar field of technology. We will use these patents as a reference later when we look at actually producing the patent application in section 2. Collecting copies that are similar to yours is important to the patent writing method we will use. So make sure you do this. Collect at least 3 patents that are similar to your idea. If you cannot find any patents you consider similar to your idea, still collect at least three that are as close to your idea as possible. One clever trick is once you have found one patent, to find similar ones, just search the patent reference number of the one you have found. If the patent you have found is cited in others, these will also come up in the search. This is a nice little cheat to quickly find other patents in your specific category to check.

Google also have their own patent search facility called 'google patents'. There is no harm in using more than one patent search engine as you may find different patents with them.

If you wish, you may pay a patent attorney to carry out the patent search for you. Depending on the attorney and the type of patent, this would typically cost around £1,000. They will be experienced in carrying out searches but in reality would be carrying out the same steps described above. If they do find similar ideas and patents they will suggest ways around these ideas in order to get your patent through the process. We will go through how to do this in section 2. Just because you have paid a patent attorney to carry out a search does not mean they will necessary find all previous art relating to your idea. They may suggest there is no similar prior art but when you pay the IPO to carry out their search, they might find something that your expert did not. Paying for expert help still has its risks.

If you find prior art that you believe will stop you obtaining a patent, you can change your design slightly or come up with an improvement on the existing art. If you can think of a way of changing your idea slightly so it does not infringe on the prior art then it may still be possible to patent your idea. If you make an improvement on the existing technology you can patent this. It may be that you are not able to manufacture the improvement without the permission of the owner of the original patent. It may be that you licence or sell the improvement to them so they can produce it. It may be that you can approach the owner of the original idea and possibly come to an agreement using your improvement to mutually benefit both parties. They may allow you to manufacture the product and in return they are also allowed to use your improvement. However you decide to proceed, it could be that you can profit from a patent that contains an improvement on an existing design.

If your search reveals that your idea does not meet one of the requirements, it may be possible to obtain another form of intellectual property protection. Your idea may be better protected with a registered design, a trademark or copyright. Even if you file for a patent you should be aware of the other forms of intellectual property protection as having multiple forms of protection is better than one. Chapter 13 explains how to obtain these alternative forms of protection. In many cases an idea is better protected with a registered design than a patent.

OTHER FORMS OF INTELLECTUAL PROPERTY PROTECTION

What intellectual property protection is best for your idea? A patent, registered design, trademark or copyright? It is important to be familiar with the other forms of protection in addition to patents. It is very likely that whatever your idea is, it will be possible to also use registered designs, trademarks and copyright to your advantage. The different uses and benefits of each type of protection are detailed below;

PATENTS

A patent protects the function of a product or a specific manufacturing process. It defines a specific scope of technology and the owner has a monopoly over its use. The owner of a patent has rights to prosecute anyone infringing on this technology. A patent is granted by a government body (in our case the IPO) and has a defined life span.

REGISTERED DESIGNS

A registered design protects the physical appearance of a product or an ornament; this includes the shape, contours, lines, colours and texture.

Compared to a patent, a registered design can be filed for a fraction of the price and for a fraction of the time and effort. It really is an easy process and this is explained in chapter 13. Whatever your idea is, as long as it has an original appearance, it is most likely worth filing a registered design, even if you are also filing for a patent. A patent will most likely take years to be granted, whereas a registered design can be filed and registered within a few weeks.

TRADEMARKS

A trademark protects your unique brand. This can be the name of your product or business. A trademark can consist of words, sounds, logos, colours or a combination of these.

There are rules to what can be registered as a trademark; these are explained in chapter 13. As with registered designs, it is likely that your idea can be protected by a trademark. Registering a trademark for your idea can add value to your idea and give you further legal protection. Having a trademark allows you to use the registered trademark symbol '®' to deter potential imitators.

COPYRIGHTS

Copyrights protect literary, dramatic, musical, illustrative, photography, computer software, web content, databases, sound, music, film and television works. Copyright protection is actually an automatic intellectual property protection. Often a product will have small print on the packaging or product itself displaying the copyright symbol ©, the name of the owner and the year. Copyrights can possibly protect the literature associated with your product including any instructions, labels and literature that will be supplied with your final product. As an example, I have published a copyright statement at the start of this book.

You should carefully consider what forms of IP are applicable to your idea and business. Further information on registered designs, trademarks and copyrights can be found in chapter 13. This includes how to file and apply them.

Now that you have carried out your initial search for prior art, you may come to the conclusion that your idea is truly original and that it is worth filing patent protection. The next chapter will outline the various steps in the patent filing process, the time scales and costs associated with patent applications. Once you are aware of these you will be in the position to decide whether to take the plunge and apply for a patent.

Chapter 4 Patent Application Process and Time Scales

Patent Process Overview

Now you have decided that filing for a patent is the right thing for your idea, it is time to understand the application process. This chapter takes you through the different stages, their costs and the time scales involved. As an overview the process consists of the following steps;

- Formal submission
- Preliminary examination
- Patent search
- Patent publication
- Substantive examination
- Granting of patent
- International filing

We will now go through each step.

Formal Submission and Preliminary Examination

Once you have put together your patent application (we will go through the process in section 2), the first thing to do is to send a copy of this to the UK Intellectual Property Office (IPO). This can be done by post or online. Once received the IPO will carry out what is known as the preliminary examination. This is an administrative check to ensure you have ticked the correct boxes, including numbering your pages correctly and using the right general format. If they spot anything wrong they will get back to you and ask you to correct your mistakes. They may give you a time frame in which to do this. Once the application is received and the preliminary examination complete, the IPO will inform you your application has been filed. They send a filing receipt, assign a patent application number and, very importantly, provide you with a filing date. This filing date is the official date from which your idea protection is enforced. It is also important as the further steps in the process have to be followed within time scales from this filing date. There is a fee of £30 associated with the initial filing. This is reduced to £20 if you carry it out online.

PATENT SEARCH

If you follow the process in this book you would have already done your own patent search. It is now the IPO's turn to carry out their official search. The patent search will set you back £150 and you have to make the request within 12 months of your filing date. The fee is reduced to £130 if filed online. The IPO will take your application and search for all related previous patent applications. They will attempt to show you several examples of previous patents with similar technology to justify why your patent can not be granted. The result of the search will be presented in the form of a report and is normally sent back to you within fourth months of receiving your request. The report is explained in further detail in chapter 12. The results of the report will indicate what prior art the examiner has found within the subject field of your idea. With the report, they will send you copies of any past patents that they believe that your application infringes on or patents that are similar to your application.

Once you receive the search report you will have an important decision to make. What next? This will depend on the content of the IPO search report and any product/

business development progress you have made in the background. If the search results are not good, i.e. the IPO examiner finds previous art that proves your idea not to be new, you can withdraw your application and make a completely new one, thus restarting the whole process. The whole patent search process is explored in more detail in chapter 12. If all is good and you are happy with the search results, you can continue the application. All being well, the IPO will automatically move things on to the publication stage as long as you do not withdraw your application.

PATENT PUBLICATION

Around 18 months after the patent filing date the IPO will publish your patent. This means your patent application will be available for the general public to see. It gives the opportunity for the general public to view and object to your application for any reason. This could prevent your patent application from being granted. It also gives the public an opportunity to potentially copy your idea. Either by just completely ripping it off or by making subtle changes to your idea which your patent application may not cover. Once your patent has been published, it is out there in the public domain forever. Also bear in mind that your details, including name and address, will be published along with the patent. This does unfortunately mean that you will have invention promotion companies chasing you. We will go into these in more detail later on in chapter 11. You will also receive several letters from scam artists asking for money in return for filing your patent in foreign countries. You have been warned! You will find information relating to these scams on the IPO website. Do not give money to anyone who is not the IPO or any other official patent office. It maybe you decide for your application not to be published, in which case write to the IPO requesting your patent withdrawal prior to publication (18 months after filing date). This can be via email. You may well also withdraw your application due to the results of the IPO patent search; we go through reasons for this in chapter 12. Assuming all goes well, your application will now move through to the substantive assessment stage.

SUBSTANTIVE ASSESSMENT

All going well you will reach the substantive assessment stage. You must file for a substantive assessment within 6 months of the patent publication date, or 18 months after the initial filing date. You will receive your official deadline for this application with the paperwork received confirming patent publication. You will now have to file form 10, along with the accompanying fees. The substantive examination costs £100, or £80 if filed for online. The substantive assessment will consist of the examiner carrying out further research into the originality of your idea. This time they take into account the original IPO search results, any objections received since the patent publication and any international searches that have been conducted (see chapter 14).

There is no specific stated response time for the IPO to carry the substantive examination. They only advise that your request is placed in a queue. Once carried out, you will either be contacted with a letter explaining when the patent will be granted, or you will receive a report explaining the objections to the application. If you receive objections you will have a set period of time to respond, usually 4 months. Within these four months you can respond to the IPO explaining why the examiners arguments are not justified. You may also amend claims to suit the objections. It may be that you need to be more specific to differentiate your idea from previous work. If you amend your claims, there is always the chance that the new claims could be rejected. At this stage, should you have objections from the IPO, I recommend getting in touch with them in the phone. They can be extremely helpful and save you a lot of time in the long run. They are particularly helpful with independent applicants, so you can decide exactly how best to change your claims. Depending on what objections they have, and how quickly they carry out the examination, this process can add a lot of time to your patent.

INTERNATIONAL APPLICATIONS

So far we have dealt with the UK IPO. If you want protection worldwide you need to consider international applications. International patent applications are covered in more detail in chapter 14. For now it is important to know what you will have to do, what the deadlines are and what the costs are. In general the whole international patent process does not have to begin until around one year from your IPO filing date. Once you start international applications things start to get expensive. So you have one year after filing your UK application to get the business side of things underway before you make decisions about international applications. There is an application form called a PCT. This has to be filed within 1 year of your UK filing date. The PCT application initiates the international patent filing process in all countries (all that will interest you at least). The PCT application will as a whole cost you around £2,500, this sum is split between a search, transmittal fee, international fee etc. See chapter 14 for the breakdown of costs. For this price you ensure that in all countries your filing date counts as the date that you originally filed your UK application. After filing your PCT, you have 18 months in which to file your patent in each country you wish to have patent protection. The PCT effectively buys you 18 months of time to decide how to proceed on an international basis. Before the 18 months are through, you must have filed patents in each country that you want protection. We will go into more detail on international patents in chapter 14. For now you need to know that you will have to take action and come up with the fees to proceed on an international basis within 12 months of your initial UK filing. This confirms the importance of having a strategy when it comes to the different time frames involved. We will go through this at the end of the chapter.

SUMMARY OF TIME LINES AND COSTS

Below is a visual time line of the actions and costs involved in patent applications. These should be considered and planned for in detail before you make your initial application.

How To File A UK Patent Yourself

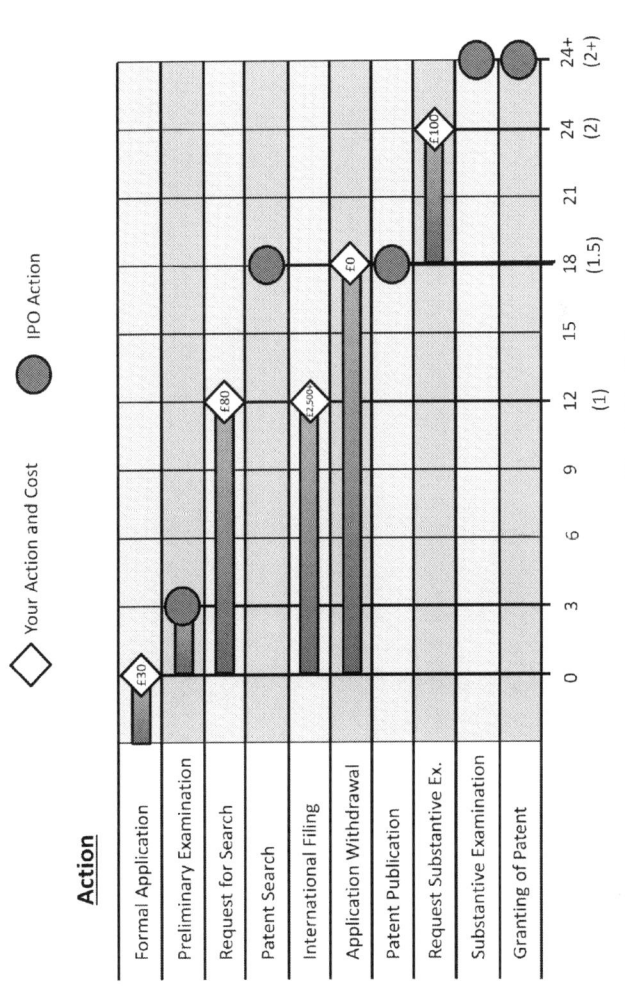

Action

Action	Time
Formal Application	£30 at 0
Preliminary Examination	~3 months
Request for Search	£80 at 12 (1)
Patent Search	~12 months
International Filing	£2,500 at 12 (1)
Application Withdrawal	£0 at 18 (1.5)
Patent Publication	~18 months (1.5)
Request Substantive Ex.	£100 at ~22
Substantive Examination	24+ (2+)
Granting of Patent	24+ (2+)

◇ Your Action and Cost   ● IPO Action

Time in Months From Filing Date (years)

43

THINGS THAT COULD AFFECT YOUR TIMING STRATEGY

Looking to license your idea? It may be worth doing some of the marketing preparation, prototyping, testing etc. prior to filing your initial UK patent. This is so you have more time to approach and negotiate with potential licensees before making the expensive decision of whether to file international patents. If you do background work before filing, you can give yourself 12 months to approach and attempt to sell your idea to manufacturers or distributors. This should be long enough to make a good assessment on whether it is worth paying out for expensive international applications.

To discover more about the world of licencing your ideas to others (manufacturers and distributors) I thoroughly recommend reading 'One Simple Idea' by Stephen Key. He is an American inventor/ designer that has been through the licensing process many times. Stephen Key proves this to be a great way of profiting from yours ideas with a manufacturer/ distributor putting in most of the effort and financial risk. You just sit back and count your earnings as they pay you a fee or percentage for each unit sold. Easy money. This could be a great low risk option for your idea.

If your plan is to manufacture your product yourself, you can use the 12 months between filing your UK patent and the international phase to produce a thorough business plan that includes quotes from potential manufactures. Once you start producing and selling your product you should have a good idea of the value that international patents could hold for your product. In chapter 11 we will go through the routes to market for your idea in more detail.

Now you should have a good idea of what the patent processes are and the costs involved. You should be able to make an informed decision on whether or not a patent is right for you. Hopefully whatever your financial position is, you have an option to file for a patent yourself by following the advice in the next chapters without incurring any excessive financial risks.

SECTION TWO: WRITING YOUR PATENT

Chapter 5 Writing Your Patent Description

Getting Ready

Now we are going to get stuck in and start producing your patent application. There are a few documents you will want close by; examples of other patent (ones that you found in chapter 3) and the IPO patents application guide. The guide is very useful and I recommend reading it before reading this chapter. It covers subjects such as the formal requirements you need to follow and it talks you through the administrative forms that must accompany your application. This chapter will go into further detail with a few more tips and tricks but the IPO guide is definitely worth a read.

Your initial application for grant of a patent will consist of the actual patent document you produce and IPO form 1, along with the £30 filing fee.

The patent application is made up of the following sections;

- Description- this will include a background, statement of invention, advantages and detailed technical description of your idea
- Drawings- Illustrating your idea
- Claims- the legal bit, outlining exactly what technology you claim to have invented.
- Abstract- an overview which is accompanied by one of your drawings.

Be sure to follow the IPO advice on formatting which can be seen on page 8 of the IPO patents application guide. We will start by producing the description.

PATENT DESCRIPTION

TITLE

Let us start with the easiest bit. The first part of the description is to give your application a title. This should, in very basic terms, describe your idea. Do not use the brand name you are planning on marketing your invention with or any other clever names, just stick to something very basic. For example if your idea is for a chocolate teapot, simply use the title 'chocolate teapot'. If your idea is indeed a chocolate tea pot, good luck to you. Also pick a title that does not give away the technology behind your idea. So if you have invented a chocolate that does not melt, there is not any need to mention this in the title. Chocolate teapot will suffice.

BACKGROUND

Now we will write the background to the idea. This sets the scene by describing the problem that your idea solves. This should be very straight forward. No need to go into great detail with facts and figures, or survey results. The severity of the problem is not in question here, keep it simple. Just describe the problem that exists, for example;

"Tea is a drink that is preferred by many to be sweetened prior to drinking. Chocolate flavouring can be used to sweeten the tea drink. Chocolate flavouring can be added to the tea by brewing the tea within a tea pot brewing vessel that is constructed with chocolate. Existing chocolate teapots available tend to melt under the high water temperatures required to brew tea. A teapot that melts causes hot liquids to spill."

This section should be use to describe the short falls of other previous inventions that are available in the same field of technology. Do this by being very specific. You should quote the patent numbers of prior art. This should be the patents that you found whilst carrying out your search in chapter 3.

It is important to demonstrate to the examiner that you are aware of what has previously been invented, as they will assume you didn't if not referenced. They will assume that your idea is therefore not new. We want to hold the examiners hand slightly and point out the prior art. This will make your application much more credible than if the examiner discovers the existing technology themselves. This will help set out how your idea is different from these previous inventions and reinforce the argument for a granted patent.

Make sure you reference patents that are as close to your technology as possible. Explain why they are similar and the differences that set yours apart as a better solution. So for the chocolate teapot example, you will need to find patents for previous chocolate teapots and explain their short falls compared to yours. So you may point out that they melt and explain why they have this short coming. For example;

"Devices have been previously proposed to infuse chocolate flavour into tea such as Pratt (US Pat. No. 51119,505463) and Toby (UK Pat. No. GB7089749). These previous devices are chocolate tea pots constructed from standard chocolate. Standard chocolate has a melting point between 30 and 32 deg C. Tea is normally brewed with water at or close to 100 deg C. This means these previous chocolate tea pot devices tended to melt and are therefore unable to contain the brewing liquid."

Apologies for the crude example but I think it shows well how the previous devices should be explained. The shortfalls in the prior art you find will most likely not be as obvious as the example, but you do need to highlight their short comings in comparison to your invention. Use very simple language and state facts. Do not use unnecessarily complex English or descriptive words. Keep it simple. Do not express your opinion by describing the previous devices in ways like "about as useful as a chocolate teapot". Instead point out the specific problems and describe the affects with words like 'adverse' or 'undesirable". Note how the previous patent applications were quoted. The surname of the inventor followed by the patent number quoted in brackets. Be sure to reference the prior art in this way. The next section of the description is the statement of invention.

STATEMENT OF INVENTION

The statement of invention should state exactly what your device can do and achieve. For example;

"This invention will enable the user to brew tea within a tea pot vessel constructed of chocolate. The tea pot is to be constructed of heat resistant chocolate. This will enable the tea pot vessel to contain liquids of up to 100 degrees Celsius without causing the chocolate construction to deform or melt. Although the heat resistance chocolate will not melt during the tea brewing process, chocolate flavours will be infused into the tea causing a desirable sweet chocolate flavour to the final brewed tea drink."

So describe what your device can achieve and how it does so. Expresses how it is different to existing devices. So in the case of the above example, the fact that the tea pot is constructed of heat resistant chocolate sets the device apart from previous devices.

ADVANTAGES

This section is used to describe your invention, how it is constructed, what it is constructed of and how it works. Here it is good to describe you invention generally, then use further paragraphs to describe it in detail using language like 'in the preferred embodiment of the invention.....' See below example for our chocolate teapot;

"The device can consist of a brewing vessel with lifting handle and spout. The top of the vessel has an opening used to insert tea and boiling water. A lid is used to cover the opening during the tea brewing process. This helps to contain the high temperatures required to optimise the tea brewing process. The preferred embodiment of the invention is to be constructed with heat resistant chocolate."

In this section also explain what elements of the idea can vary such as materials used and the shape. This could include anything that would not affect the function of the device. For example you may wish to state items such as below;

"The main tea brewing vessel of the tea pot can be of any shape."

Remember the patent covers how your device functions, not the visual design. Therefore do not describe anything that is purely related to how the product looks and is not essential to how the device functions. If you have ideas as to what the final product will look like, we will protect this later with a registered design (see chapter 13). Filing registered designs is a much simpler and quicker process than filing your patent applications.

The next part is the detailed description. In this section we will make reference to the patent application drawings. Therefore it is best to produce the drawings first so we will go through this first in the following chapter.

Chapter 6 Producing Your Patent Drawings

Drawing Method

Your patent drawings come after your detailed description in the application. To produce the detailed description, it is easiest to reference your drawings. So we will produce the patent drawings first. The ideal way to produce your patent drawings is to use CAD (computer Aided Design) software.

If you do not have any CAD software there are several packages you can download for free such as 'Solid Edge'. If you are not confident or familiar with how to use the software, there are many online tutorials you can find on youtube. Personally I am an engineer by trade so use CAD every day at work. The software I use is autoCAD by Autodesk. If you wish you can get a 30 day free trial of their software which should be more than enough time to learn and draw your own patent drawings. There are many youtube videos to help you should you get stuck. Patent drawings are fairly basic due to the legal requirements. This means there is no fancy 3D rendering or even greyscale shading permitted. For this reason I would recommend giving the CAD option a go, even if you have no experience with this. If you are still not keen on using any CAD software, fear not, good old fashioned hand drawn illustrations are perfectly acceptable for your application.

Format

Patent drawings have to follow some formatting guidelines. These are stated on page 10 of the IPO application guide, under the heading 'Dos and DONTs'. Make sure you follow these rules. Your drawings do have to be fairly basic in that they are to be in black and white (including no grey scale shading), have no descriptive writing on them, to be on A4 page size etc. The various parts of your idea should be labelled with numbers only and you will reference these numbers in your detailed description.

PRODUCING DRAWING BY HAND

If you decide to produce your drawings by hand, I would first recommend making sure you have the right tools for the job. Make sure you have a good quality drawing pen. This could be a black fine line fibre tip pen. I recommend using a 0.3mm tip, you should be able to get one for a few pounds at a stationary shop or an online store. You can sketch your idea first in pencil to establish ideas of how the finished drawings will look.

One method that I have used is to first sketch in pencil, and then draw over this with your drawing pen neatly using a ruler for straight lines. Now with care, rub out the pencil to leave just the black ink visible, or trace the drawing onto a fresh piece of paper. You can do this by placing the fresh paper on top of the sketch and place both on a glass table or window. With the glass table you may have to put a light source under it in order to trace. With the window, make sure there it is sufficient daylight (apologies this should be obvious). Now you can trace onto the fresh paper neatly ensuring the drawing is located where you want it on the new paper. Plan if you want other drawings on the same sheet and allow room for the component number labels, the required margins at all sides of the page (20mm top and left, 15mm right and 10mm bottom), the title and sheet numbers.

There is no point squeezing too much on one sheet so plan ahead.

Different Views

Whether you use CAD or free hand your drawings, your drawings must capture certain requirements. You will most likely require several views of your device in order to capture all the features. So as a general rule you will need to include as many views of your invention as necessary to be able to fully describe all its features. You may also need to include section drawings, or exploded drawings depending on your device. Each feature will need to be labelled. You are to do this by numbering each component/ feature etc.

The next section covers the detailed description and in this you will be referring to the numbers labelled on your drawings. You may need to go back after writing your description to add labels or additional views of your idea to fully enable you to describe everything in detail.

Drawing Examples

See below simple examples of the different views that you can use. Be sure to use enough different views to fully describe your idea. The first page of diagrams also shows some of the formal administration requirements. Note the drawings are to be on A4 sized paper as per all the other pages in your patent application.

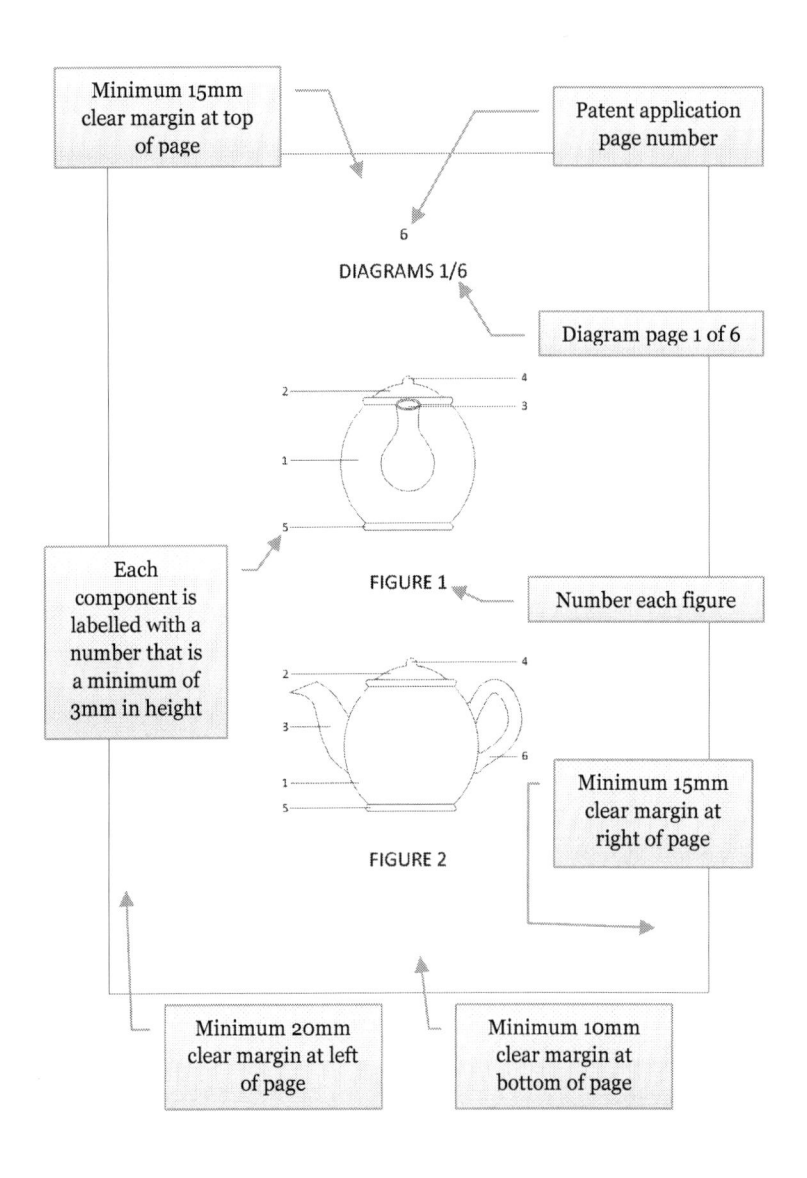

How To File A UK Patent Yourself

- Minimum 15mm clear margin at top of page
- Patent application page number

6

DIAGRAMS 1/6

Diagram page 1 of 6

FIGURE 1

Number each figure

Each component is labelled with a number that is a minimum of 3mm in height

FIGURE 2

Minimum 15mm clear margin at right of page

Minimum 20mm clear margin at left of page

Minimum 10mm clear margin at bottom of page

7
DIAGRAMS 2/6

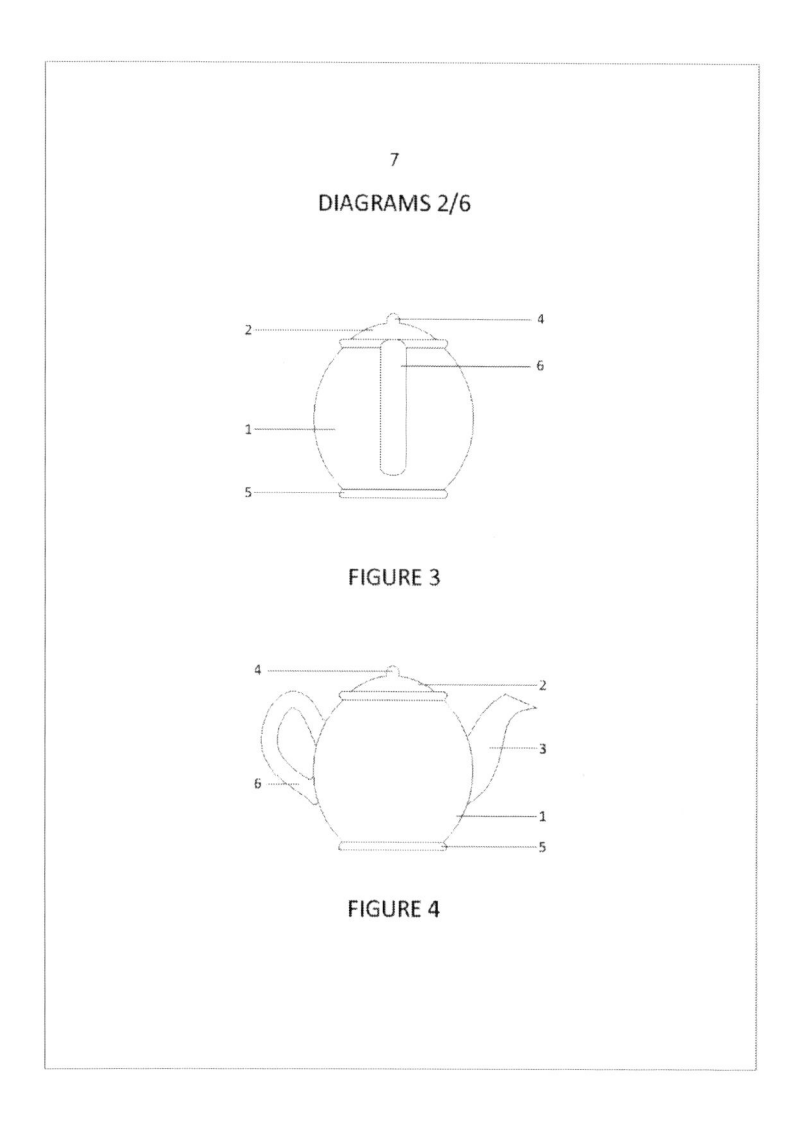

FIGURE 3

FIGURE 4

8
DIAGRAMS 3/6

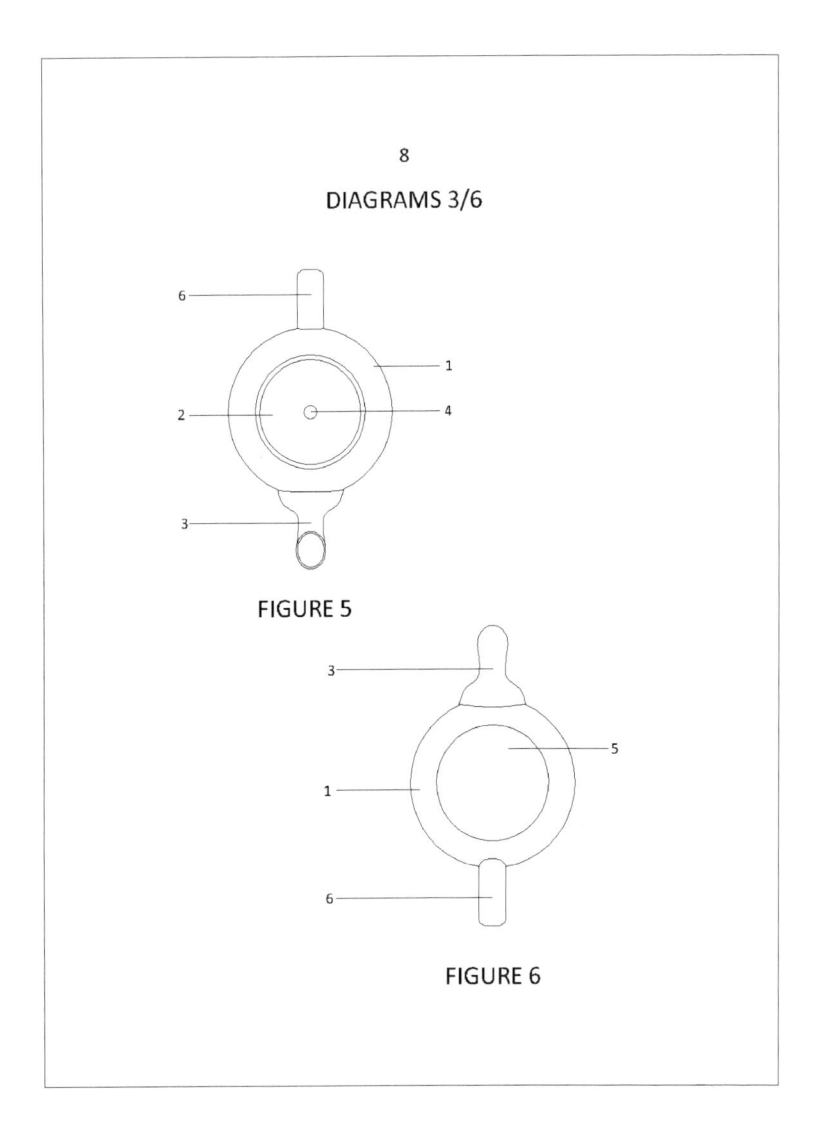

FIGURE 5

FIGURE 6

9
DIAGRAMS 4/6

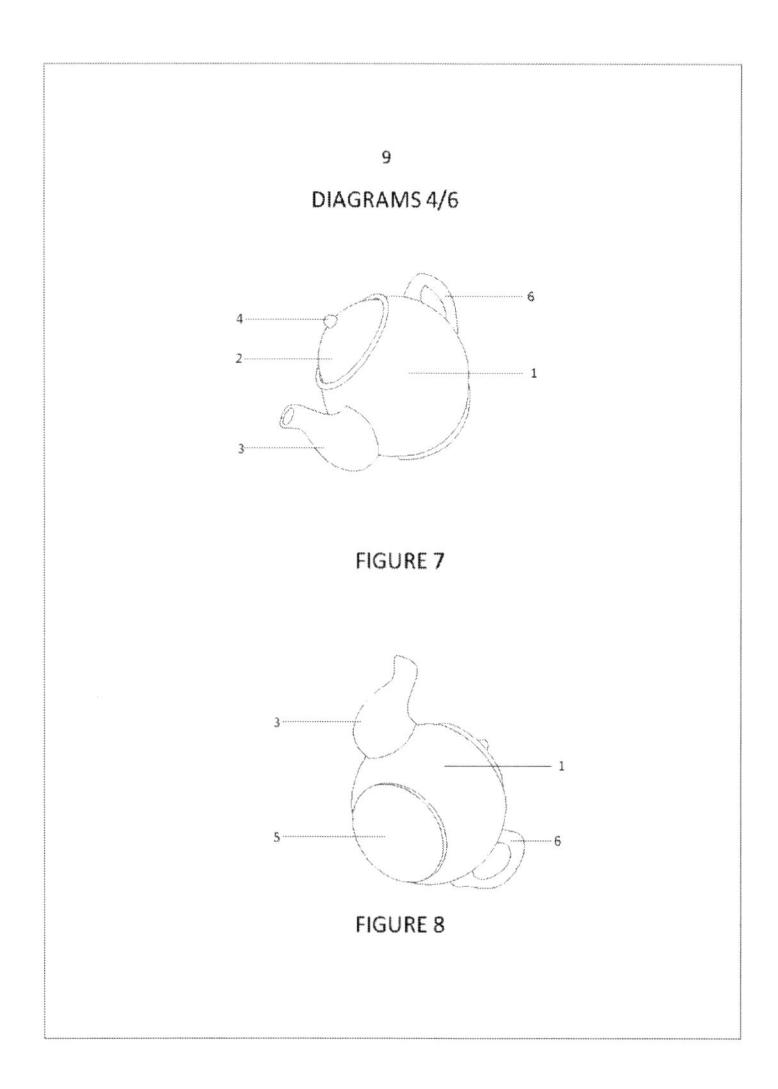

FIGURE 7

FIGURE 8

10

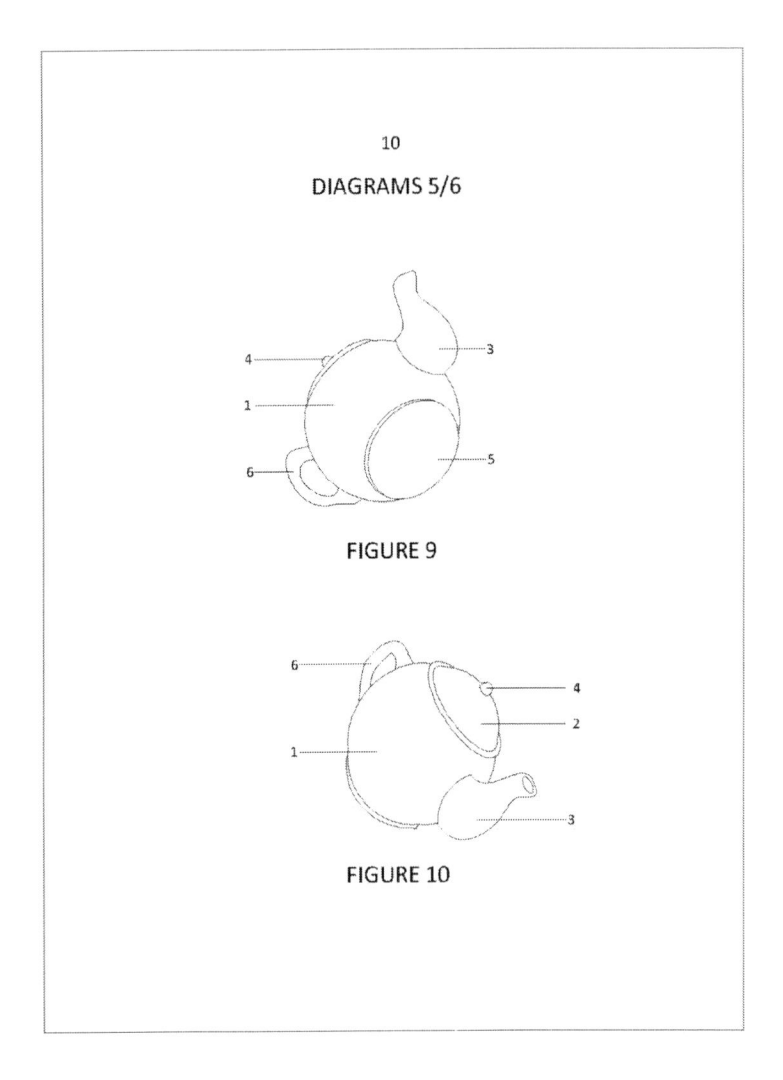

DIAGRAMS 5/6

FIGURE 9

FIGURE 10

11
DIAGRAMS 6/6

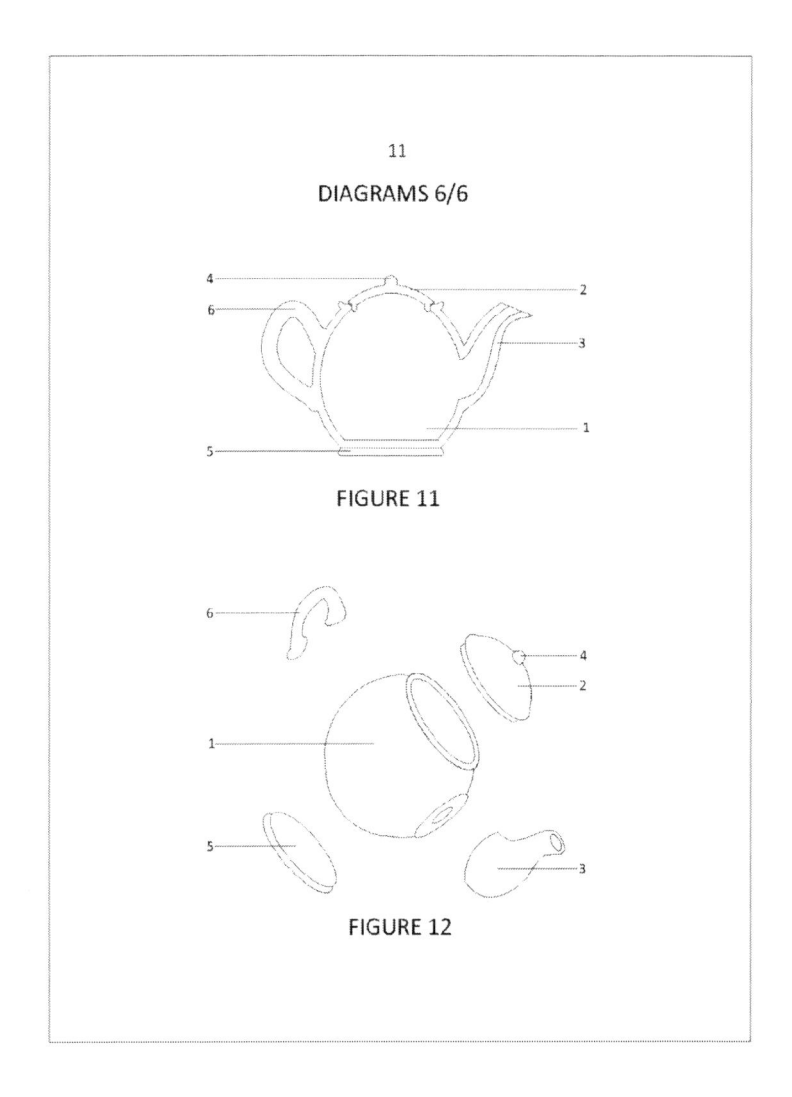

FIGURE 11

FIGURE 12

CHAPTER 7 WRITING YOUR DETAILED DESCRIPTION

Now we will go through the requirements of the detailed description. Here the object is to describe your invention so that someone would be able to replicate it. We will expand on the description in the advantages section and this time use references to our drawings.

The detailed description can be started as follows;

"The invention will now be described by the way of example and reference to the accompanying drawings in which;

Figure 1 shows a front view of the chocolate teapot

Figure 2 shows a right side view of the chocolate teapot

Figure 3 shows a back view of the chocolate teapot

Figure 4 shows a left side view of the chocolate teapot

Figure 5 shows a top view of the chocolate teapot

Figure 6 shows a bottom view of the chocolate teapot

Figure 7 shows a top right view of the chocolate teapot

Figure 8 shows a bottom right view of the chocolate teapot

Figure 9 shows a bottom left view of the chocolate teapot

Figure 10 shows a top left view of the chocolate teapot

Figure 11 shows a section view of the chocolate teapot

Figure 12 shows an exploded view of the chocolate teapot"

You will also need to include any drawings that include alternative forms of your invention.

It is very unlikely that you will require all the different views shown above. You only need to include as many views as required in order to fully explain your idea. These have been shown to suggest what each view would look like and what to call each view.

Next you want to start the detailed description with reference to the drawings. The trick here is to describe your invention enough to explain how it works but also vaguely enough so as wider range of technology is protected. This is a fine balance as the IPO will not grant a patent on a specification that is too vague but if you are too specific it may limit you to what your patent actually protects. Also if you are too vague you are likely to infringe on previously patented technology which will stop your efforts being granted.

A good thing to do is to be fairly specific with your idea and then expand on this by suggesting alternative forms of your idea that differ slightly. These can all be documented and form a part of your application and therefore also be protected. This may involve suggesting different materials and different forms that the idea can take on.

EXAMPLE DETAILED DESCRIPTION

Your description should contain references to the drawings with the use of the number labels as per the below example;

"The lid 2 can be lifted using the lid handle 4. Boiling water and tea are poured into the brewing vessel 2. The lid 2 is then put back in place for the brewing period. During the brewing period, the chocolate flavour is infused into the tea from the vessel 2 which is made from heat resistant chocolate. Once brewed the tea pot can be lifted with the handle 6 and the chocolate flavour infused tea is poured through the spout 3 and into a drinking vessel."

Include detail alternative forms of your idea as per the example below;

"Alternatively the chocolate teapot can be constructed using a metallic material such as stainless steel or a ceramic material. The vessel 2 can be lined with chocolate that allows the chocolate flavour to infuse into the tea during the brewing process."

You should describe every item labelled in the drawings. You can reference a label number as many times as necessary to explain your idea. Again it is important to describe as many alternative forms of your idea. The different forms and variations of your idea should also have associated drawings. The alternatives should detail features which are not necessarily essential to your device but could possibly be of benefit. You want to cover as many ideas like this as you can because if you don't, someone else could attempt to patent the improvements for their selves at a later date. This could stop you using such improvements without the improvement inventor's permission. It could also be that someone files a patent of a slight deviation to your idea which enables them to get around the technology covered by your patent, and produce a similar product, or a product with the same advantages as yours. With this in mind, you should think of as many different embodiments of your invention as you can and include these within your application.

Chapter 8 Writing Your Patent Claims

The claims are the most vital section of your application to get exactly right. These will form the legal basis of your intellectual property protection. The other sections are there solely to support the claims. The claims spell out exactly what technology you are protecting. With a little knowledge and some examples, there is no reason why you cannot produce your own claims to protect your idea.

Claims format

To produce your claims you have to follow a few rules with regards to the English, formatting and content used. Some worth noting are as follows;

Each claim is to be numbered

Each claim must be a single sentence, no full stops are allowed.

A claim must not make any commercial claims or anything that is not essential to the inventions function.

Formulating your claims

Your first claim (claim 1) should describe your invention very broadly and then you can file dependant claims which refer to an earlier claim. So your first claim should describe your invention as broadly as possible. You can then narrow down further details in dependant claims that refer back to your claim 1. The claims set out exactly what technology your patent covers. So, broader claims will cover a greater field of technology. However, the claim must be new so a broader claim is more likely to infringe on existing technology. Also the examiners at the IPO may not accept extremely broad claims and may ask you to narrow them down making them more specific. So your first claim should be as broad as possible without infringing on any existing patents.

Your following claims can refer back to the first claim but highlight different features that you wish to protect. These dependant claims can stop others from modifying your invention slightly and trying to patent that. So think of as many things as possibile to cover with your dependant claims in order to protect as much as you can with your patent. We can withdraw these claims at a later date if the patent office is not happy with them or believes they are obvious. For example, putting two handles on your chocolate tea pot instead of one may be considered obvious.

Legally a claim must be a single sentence. So stick to this. We will go through some example claims to explain how this is achieved.

A claim must not make any commercial claims or anything that is not technical. For example you must not say that the invention will make loads of money. Also do not provide any sort of loose opinion on your idea, for example do not say that this invention is tremendously better than all other inventions.

USE CLAIMS FROM OTHER PATENTS AS A TEMPLATE

Now is the time to read the claims set out in the patents you found in chapter 3. You can copy the style of English used so that yours follows the correct format. Note that someone probably paid a patent attorney a lot of money to produce those claims. After reading several sets of claims and the examples in the IPO guide you should make your first attempts at drafting yours. Remember to keep them as vague as possible but also they have to be original so some detail is necessary. The first claim can be followed by other claims that add to the first or describe slightly different forms of the invention.

At this stage do not worry too much about including dependant claims that you think will not be accepted, you will have opportunities later to change/ remove these from the application.

EXAMPLES OF CLAIMS

Below are examples of claims;

1. Chocolate flavoured drinking tea can be produced by brewing traditional tea within a chocolate teapot constructed using heat resistant chocolate.
2. Alternative to claim 1, the teapot can be constructed of stainless steel with a chocolate lined internal brewing vessel.
3. Alternative to claim 1, the chocolate teapot can have two spouts in order to fill two drinking vessels simultaneously whilst pouring the brewed chocolate tea.

Your claims will most likely be longer and contain more information than the above examples, but these give you a good idea of where to start. Make sure to study the similar patents you found during your search. Remember that the example patents you found in your search were most likely produced by a professional patent attorney, so learn from the language and format they used. These example patents contain great examples of ideas similar to yours so use them wisely.

Chapter 9 Writing Your Abstract

The last section of the patent to produce is the abstract. The abstract is a paragraph containing the main details of the patent content. It is the first thing people will see if they have carried out a patent search and found your patent. It should give the reader a good idea of the technology covered by the document and enable the reader to judge whether or not it is worth while reading the rest of the application. To create the abstract, first state the title of your idea, followed by a brief description referencing the numbering on one of your drawings. The abstract is to also include one of your drawings. It is recommended to pick the drawing that best summarises the idea as a whole, quote this at the end of your abstract. Example abstract;

"Chocolate teapot

The device is a chocolate teapot used to brew chocolate flavoured drinking tea. The vessel 1, lid 2, spout 3, and base 5 are all constructed of heat resistant chocolate. Boiling water and tea leaves are poured into the brewing vessel 1. Chocolate flavouring infuses into the brewing tea from the chocolate vessel 1. The brewed chocolate tea is then poured out of the vessel 1 via the spout 3 by lifting and tilting the teapot with handle 6.

Additionally, the vessel 1 can be constructed of an alternative material such as stainless steel or a ceramic material and the vessel 1 lined with chocolate.

Additionally, the chocolate teapot can have two spouts 3 to allow the user to pour two chocolate flavoured tea drinks at once.

Figure 4 is to accompany the abstract."

You could use this as a template or use an abstract from one of the other patents you have read.

Chapter 10 Formatting your Application

Order of Sections

Now we need to get your application ready for submitting to the IPO. First thing we must do is put the different sections into the right order. The sections must be organised as follows with each section starting on a new page;

- Abstract
- Description, which includes; background, statement of invention, advantages and detailed description
- Drawings
- Claims

Formatting Rules

Stick to the formatting rules. These are on the IPO application guide page 8. Each page must be numbered, single sided A4 size, black and white only, use margins that are 2cm a minimum on all sides, number each page at the top in the centre. The drawing pages to be numbered diagrams 1/6, diagrams 2/6, etc. to suit how many pages you have, as per the example drawings featured. Do not include trademarks, names or fictitious words.

Once you have you put your application together, you should get someone to read it over for you. This is to pick up any spelling or grammatical errors. The person you ask does not necessarily have to be anyone who has experience with filing patents.

And that is it. That is your patent document completed. Well done and take a well-deserved break.

FORMS AND PAYMENTS

To submit your patent application to the IPO, you must ensure that you also submit the correct forms and fees. Your initial application must include the IPO Patents form 1- Request for grant of a patent, this form is fairly straight forward to complete. Your personal details are required. You are required to give a title for your invention. Keep this simple; the title does not need to describe the invention in great detail or why it is new or unique. If you are following this guide you will not need to fill in any agent details, priority dates or divisional applications. You need to state whether or not you are the sole inventor or if there are other inventors.

There is a £30 application fee to pay when you file form 1. This is reduced to £20 if you file online and pay the fee at the same time. You have to state the number of sheets you are submitting for each section of your patent. You can at this point file a request for search form 9a, but note you have 12 months to do this. The request for search costs £150 or £130 if done online so you may wish to have a think about this before you apply. The request for search is covered in more detail in chapter 12.

Section Three: After Your Initial Application

Chapter 11 Prototypes, testing and commercial analysis

Prototypes

Although filing your own patent will hopefully not break the bank, we still need to bear in mind it will require the investment of time and effort. With this in mind you want to be sure your idea actually works. Also we need to be sure that the idea is actually commercially viable, so can it actually be manufactured and sold for a reasonable profit. This chapter explores these tests so you can be confident that filing for a patent is the right thing to do, from practical and commercial points of view.

Your first prototype(s) will be produced to prove your idea actually works and functions correctly. You will probably want to do this soon after your initial eureka moment. There are many ways of going about this. It maybe that you produce a prototype that may not look the part, but does enough to prove the technlogy works. This can be made from anything you can get your hands on. Once made, you may have proved your new idea works, or that you need to tweak a few things first. Either way you probably are best testing your idea works before filing any intellectual property, as you do not want to waste any of your precious time.

Once you have proved the function of your idea you will probably want to assess its commercial potential. This aspect is explored later in the chapter. You can also take your prototyping further to produce something that looks eye catching, more like the finished product would look. This may be so you can decide on your ideas best possible form to help you market the idea. You may wish to gauge interest from potential investors or distributors/ retailers prior to having expensive moulds produced. A prototype that is produced for visual impact may not function as the finished product would, but will show how the finished product would look and feel.

A good low cost way of representing the final look of your product is to use a Computer Aided Design (CAD) package. This could be 2D or a 3D rendered model. As stated previous when we looked at producing the patent, there are many different software packages out there, most of which will give you a free 30-day trial. Also there are many online tutorial videos that are free to view which explain the basics. Sketch-up is a 3D Cad software package that you can download for free. So it may be worth a try at least, even if you have no experience with 3D CAD. I recommend going on YouTube and watching some of the free tutorials, you may well enjoy giving it a go and pick up a new skill.

Alternatively, if you are not confident with doing this yourself, you can hire someone to do this for you. There are websites which offer the services of free-lance designers for relatively low cost rates. Just put freelance graphic designers into your internet search engine and many will pop up. There are website such as fiverr.com and Elance that specialise on one-off contract works like this. You may wish to go with someone local; there seems to be a lot of choice out there. I have not used any if these myself but understand they can give an excellent service.

One method of prototyping that has come on a long way in recent years is 3D printing. A 3D printer can turn a 3D CAD model into a real solid object. I have used companies that allow you to upload your CAD model to their website. They then 3D print your model in whatever material you wish, and post the prototype to you. If you have a 3D CAD model of your idea, there is no reason you cannot do this yourself. You can upload your model and get instant quotes for 3d prints in a range of different materials. The website I used was actually based in Belgium. I uploaded my 3D model and the online software highlighted problem areas of the model that were too thin for 3D printing. It was easy to them adjust this and the finished product sent was excellent. I then spray painted the model to finish it, some companies will do this for you for an additional charge.

COMMERCIAL ASSESSMENTS

It is all well having your big idea and protecting your intellectual property, but what you really want is to make a few bob out of it. So how do you do this? There are several options here. You will have to decide on what method to apply by the type of idea you have and the time and money you wish to invest.

Once you have decided that your idea works through prototyping, it is a good idea to access its commercial value prior to investing your time into the patent process. You may have a fantastic idea, but if it will cost thousands to produce each unit, or is difficult to sell as it may have a small market, it may not be commercially viable. Hopefully your product is easy and cheap to produce and will sell for a huge mark up. It would be wise to first confirm this prior to spending valuable time developing and filing the intellectual property. For this reason I would recommend conducting an initial analysis that should involve thinking about the following factors;

- Approximate material cost- are low or high cost materials required?
- Manufacturing technique required- research typical costs for the manufacturing method you believe is required. This may include tooling costs for moulds, or equipment costs if you wish to produce the product yourself. If you are not sure how it would be manufactured, research how similar products are produced.
- Cost of packaging.
- Market size for your product.
- Cost of similar products if available. Possible product selling price.
- How much profit you can make on each sale? If you are selling direct you may have marketing costs. If selling to retailers or wholesalers or distributors, you can expect to give them a 40% or 60% discount on the retail price respectively.

You can conduct this initial analysis yourself. I suggest that you do this before you file for your patent and/or other IP. Then after you have your IP filing under way, you have a head start with regards to getting your project underway. Also if you decide to contact any investors, the first thing they will ask is about your projected financial figures. They are more interested in the potential margins than how great your idea is so have your figures all sorted out before any discussions. If you have ever watched the Dragon's Den you will be familiar with inventors getting carried away with their ideas and forgetting to pay attention to business aspects.

ROUTES TO MARKET

To further access the commercial potential of your product you will need to consider the different route to market options. There are some listed below;

-Self-manufacture

-Outsourcing manufacture

-Licensing

-Assignment

SELF-MANUFACTURE

If you decide to self-manufacture your product, you will need to get quotations for the materials and equipment required. You will then be able to come to a reasonable estimate of cost per unit considering a certain batch size. You should also consider how to distribute your product. It may be that you supply local retailers. You should bear in mind here that most retailers will expect to purchase the product for around a 40% discount from the price they will be selling at. This will vary with different retailers and different types of products. If you wish to sell directly to a distributor or wholesaler, they typically would expect around a 60% discount off the retail price. Again this figure will be different for different products and vary between differet distributors but can be used as a figure to carry out your commercial analysis.

Another option is to use a fulfilment service. An example of this would be to use a company such as Amazon. You can have you product stored in the Amazon warehouse, advertised on their website, and delivered by them. They take the money off the customers then pass it on to you after taking a fee for themselves. You may decide to distribute the product yourself. You could do this by making a website and taking online orders, or advertising and telesales etc. It is fairly straight forward now days to create a website capable of taking orders and payments. Examples of companies that can host such websites are yahoo and 1&1.com.

OUTSOURCING MANUFACTURE

You may decide to outsource manufacture. You would then need to get quotations from contract manufactures. You should be able to find contract manufacturers that specialise in the sector of products that your idea belongs to by using an internet search engine. They will be able to quote for everything from initial tooling costs, to packaging and shipping. There are companies in the UK that can handle outsourcing of manufacturing to countries such as China, which is helpful if you are not confident in dealing with companies where language barriers can cause communication problems. Similarly you may not trust overseas companies with your intellectual property as places like China are notorious for ignoring intellectual property rights. Make sure you have at least an NDA in place prior to talking to a manufacturer and better still some IP. You can let them know that your idea is patent pending if you have filed for a patent, or quote your registered design number if you have one.

If you are still worried about people using your idea, you could ask for quotations that are for slightly modified versions of your product. It maybe that you change an important feature of your product in order to keep it a secret, whilst still keeping the product a similar size and complexity. This allows you to get fairly accurate quotations for things like tooling, and production costs, without actually giving your idea away.

LICENSING

Another option is to license out your invention. This is renting out your idea to a manufacturer or distributor by granting them permission to produce and sell your idea. In return, the manufacturer pays you a small amount for each product sold. A licensing agreement would usually consist of an assignment fee paid at the start of the agreement to you and a royalty fee paid for each unit sold. The royalty fee is normally calculated as a percentage of the wholesale price per unit. So for every unit the manufacturer or distributor sells you will earn a royalty of around 2 to 10 percent. This percentage will depend on the product and the agreement you manage to negotiate.

The advantage of licensing your idea is that the manufacturer traditionally pays for the initial upfront costs that include tooling and setup. They will also manage and pay for the marketing and distribution. This is an advantage as they are likely to have the retail contacts required to generate large sales figures. You should do your research before attempting to license out any ideas and I would thoroughly recommend you read Stephen Key's book "One Simple Idea". Stephen Key is an American inventor who has much experience licensing out his ideas to companies and his book talks you through his tried and tested method. He talks you through how to find appropriate manufactures, how to approach them with cold calling techniques and how to present your ideas on an information sell sheet.

I would recommend filing your own intellectual property as per the guidance in this book and then licensing out of your idea as a low upfront cost way of profiting from your invention. Licensing will also cut down on the time you spend on managing the manufacturing, distribution and marketing processes if this does not interest you. You will make less profit per product sold but have less time and money invested. It is also likely that you will achieve a much larger number of sales, in a much shorter time frame, than if you managed the whole manufacturing yourself.

Assignment

Assignment is when you sell the rights to your idea completely. You assign the intellectual property to another person or company. This can happen if you develop an idea that fits nicely into a manufacturer's product line. You will want to first have a good idea of what minimum price you want for your idea. So you need to work out how much it is worth to yourself and to the company you are selling to.

If like me you have many ideas I would recommend analysing them all commercially prior to investing time and money on a chosen one. If your goal is to maximise profit, it may not be your favourite idea, or most technically advanced idea, that you pursue. It is likely to be the easiest and cheapest to manufacture that will bring you the most financial success. You will need to consider marketing costs and target market size to have any idea of the possible profits involved.

CHAPTER 12 REQUEST FOR SEARCH

FORMS AND COSTS

Now that you have filed an initial patent application and considered the commercial aspects to your idea, it is time to think about pushing forward the patent application. After filing your patent you will have 12 months to request a search. This involves paying the IPO to search for prior art, similar to the exercise we went through in chapter 3. This time a professional patent attorney working for the IPO will be attempting to find anything that could stop your patent from being granted. Fear not. If they do find something you still have some options that we will go through later in this chapter.

Requesting a search is a fairly simple exercise, you fill in form 9a (request for search) and pay the appropriate fee. This form needs to be filed within 12 months of your initial request for grant of patent (filling date). The cost for the search request is £150 by post or £130 online. You should now know from the commercial analysis in the last chapter, whether or not it is worth your time and money to carry through the patent process and pay the search fee.

Even if you have conducted your own search as per chapter 3, there is still a chance that the IPO patent examiner will find some prior art related to your patent that you were not aware of, so there is still risk that your application won't be successful. As long as you haven't found any clearly similar prior art you think will stop your application, my advice would be to go for it and request the search.

After you submit form 9a and the appropriate fees, you have to wait for the IPO to carry out the search. They advise that this should take no longer than 6 months. In my experience this can take a little longer. It may be worth ringing them to check on the progress of your search if you have been waiting a long time. It appears they pile up the applications as they come in and assess them one by one from the top. After ringing them in the past my application has magically risen to the top of the pile as it was actioned shortly after.

Once again I stress that the IPO seem to handle calls extremely efficiently and they are very helpful. I have always had a friendly sounding voice at the end of the phone and they will put you through to the actual examiners that review your application and they in turn are extremely helpful. There is no reason not to take full advantage of this.

SEARCH REPORT

The IPO will get back to you and provide you with a search report. The report can be a little confusing. There is a table of items with each item being coded. They also send through copies of the prior art found. This prior art will be copies of previously filed patents for similar technology. Even if your patent differs greatly from anything previously filed the IPO will still send to you copies of the most similar patents that they can find and possibly refer to them within the search report.

The search report will consist of a covering letter and a table with and print outs of the prior art that is referenced in the table. The table will contain several items. Each item refers to one or more of your claims, the reason they are flagged-up (categorised X, Y or A), and the reference to prior art.

Refer to the IPO application guide page 26 for an example of the search results table that you will receive.

Each item raised in your search report is there for a reason. The reason relates to the category flagged up. The meanings of each category are as follows;

Category X- documents that indicate lack of novelty or inventive step. This will stop your patent application from progressing.

Category Y- Documents that indicate lack of inventive step if combined with one or more documents of the same category. This will also stop your application progressing.

Category A- Document indicating technological background and/or state of the art. This means that the prior art found will not stop your patent application. They patent office include past patents of similar inventions in your product category for your information.

You will receive a copy of the prior art referenced so you can review why this has been sited.

NEXT STEPS

You now have several options to carefully consider. If the search results received contain multiple category X and Y items, it may be that you decide not to continue the application. It is unlikely you will receive a granted patent for this idea as the IPO have deemed it unoriginal. The search I had carried out for my drink chiller idea came back with a number of items referenced as category X and Y. I could see why the examiner raised these items but I could also see why my idea was different. I had not explained clearly enough the differences between existing technology and my idea. There were clear differences so I withdrew my application and re-filed it. This time I highlighted the clear differences and advantages of my idea. I referenced the prior art patents mentioned in the search report and clearly explained in the new specification how my idea was different. This was fairly straight forward to do once the prior art is presented and so highlights the importance of carrying out a thorough search before filing your initial application.

If you re-file within 12 months of the original application, you can still maintain your initial filing date. So if the IPO search results are not the best, you can change your application to suit and re-send as long as you are within the 12 month deadline.

If all goes well the only items raised in the search report will be classified as category A. The items raised will not stop the grant of a patent and you can continue the application. It may be that items raised as category X or Y are minor issues. You can argue these at the substantive examination stage and present a case as to why your claims are original and contain an inventive step. You may be asked to adjust your claims slightly at the substantive examination stage which we will go through in chapter 14.

Assuming you do not withdraw your application, your patent will be published approximately 18 months after the initial filing date. Publication means your application is available for the general public to view. It will be published onto the same databases that you conducted your initial patent searches. It also means that some of your details will be published, such as your name and address (or business name and address). If there is any reason why you would not want the information contained within the application available for public viewing, you may wish to consider withdrawing at this point.

If you are not confident of getting your application approved based on the search report, you may also wish to withdraw your application. The idea you have come up with will now go public and therefore will be there for people to copy if you do not follow through getting the patent granted. You can withdraw your application at this stage and re-file it with added information or changed claims, based on the results of the search report.

I myself withdrew and changed an application at this stage. This was due to the IPO search report saying my application was not novel and with prior art to show this. The prior art sent included several patent applications from the distant past that had drawings that looked loosely similar to mine. My ideas were significantly different to the prior art sent. I withdraw my initial application and filed a new one quoting the prior art the examiner found. I stressed the differences in my new application and made the new technology a lot clearer. This was a good opportunity to improve on my first application and the next search results I got back were clean of any category X and Y items.

After publication, you are guaranteed to be contacted by invention promotion companies and agents. They will offer to assess the commercial viability of your idea and assist with finding a manufacturer to license the idea. Be very wary of these companies. They will write to you personally praising your amazing idea and promising the world in royalty payments should you use their services. They will normally offer to carry out an assessment of the commercial viability, which they may charge a large fee for. They may also offer to approach manufacturers for you in return for a fee and a percentage of royalty payments.

I was approached by one such company who said they knew manufacturers that were interested in my idea. They wanted several thousand pounds just to approach and negotiate a licensing contract with them. They wanted the money upfront with no guarantee that a deal would be made. There seemed to be no incentive for them to actually close a deal once they have your money other than a very small percentage of the royalty fee. I responded to the offer stating I would be willing to increase the royalty fee after a deal was made if they were willing to wave the initial engagement fee. They were not interested in this which just shows after all the talk they were not willing to put their money where their mouth was. I am sure there are legitimate agents out there, but I would be very careful about engaging with any that want any large upfront fee which shows a complete lack of confidence they have of closing a deal for you.

Before you do engage with potential licensees, agents or manufacturers, you also want to look at the other forms of intellectual protection available to you. These are covered in the next chapter.

CHAPTER 13 OTHER FORMS OF INTELLECTUAL PROPERTY

As explored in chapter 3, there are other forms of intellectual property and it is important to consider which ones are right for your idea. As far as intellectual property goes, the more forms of protection you have the better. You may file for a patent to protect the way your idea functions, a registered design to protect the physical appearance, a trademark to protect your brand name and copyright to protect the product literature or marketing material. It may be that a patent is not right for your product. Sometimes a registered design or copyright is a better choice. Below are details of registered designs, trademarks, copyrights and how to file for or use them.

REGISTERED DESIGNS

A registered design protects the shape and appearance of a product. It can stand alongside a patent in protecting your idea. Where the patent protects the function and how your idea works, the registered design protects the visual appearance. You can use registered design protection in addition to patent protection for your ideas. This could benefit you for example, if someone was to create a similar product that functioned in a slightly different way, they would not be permitted to use the same design that you have registered.

If the appearance of your idea is key to how it functions, or you believe it will be key to you products appeal, it may be more prudent to use the protection of a registered design instead of a patent all together. A registered design has advantages over a patent. It is cheaper to file and is significantly less time consuming to follow through to approval. The protection can last up to 25 years, on the condition that renewal fees are paid every 5 years. The initial filing fee and first 5 years of protection costs £60. The renewal fees are paid every 5 years after the initial filing with the first renewal costing £130, increasing each time with the fourth renewal costing £450. If you decide to file more than one design at once the fee decreases slightly. Registering additional designs in the same application will cost £40 for each additional design.

You can pay the IPO to perform a design search. They search their database of existing registered designs for a fee of £25. To request this you need to fill in form DF21. You do not necessarily need to request the search. It may however, save you some money if they do find anything, as you will know not to attempt to register the design or you may wish to change your design to suit the search results if something is found.

CRITERIA FOR REGISTERED DESIGN

For your design to be successfully registered it must meet the following criteria. It must be original, there must not be any designs previously filed similar to yours. This means that the appearance, shape and decoration of your idea must be different from any previously filed designs. On top of this, the examiners will also search for any products they can find (with a registered design or not) that are similar to yours. The examiners will carry out a similar search exercise to a patent search to ensure that your design is new.

HOW TO FILE FOR A REGISTERED DESIGN

Filing for your registered design is fairly straight forward. You need to get form DF2A from the IPO website. The form comes with guidance notes which you should read carefully. You need to fill in the form and provide the required illustrations of your product. The illustrations can take the form of photographs; this could be of a prototype. The illustrations can also be drawings, hand drawn or CAD. When I have registered designs I used 3D CAD illustrations but this is not a requirement. It is good to send in drawings or photos that show all the different views of your design. Be sure to capture all the important features of your idea. There are certain rules that you must stick to. For example, you are not allowed any writing to feature on your designs. This means that labels shown on the product are not permitted. If you use multiple illustrations to describe your design, these must all be in the same format, i.e, all 3D rendered CAD images, or all photographs etc.

The design registration forms have a small section in which you can describe a limited amount of features such as the colour and the materials used. You can also specify that these are not important. I would recommend this as it will increase the scope covered by your registered design.

After you have sent in your application with the forms and fees you need to wait for the IPO to get back to you. There is an option to register the design but not have it published till a later date. This may be a good option for you if you have a patent application going through, and you do not wish for people to see your design. Your design may give away technical aspects that you may not want disclosed until your patent application has progressed further. You may not want to have the design published until you have the product to market or have completed your product testing. To defer publication of your design, you simply fill in the correct section of the DF2A form. You then later send in form DF2C with the appropriate fee and request for publication for the registered design to be formalised. You can defer the registration of your design for up to 12 months. A deferred design does not have the same level of protection as a registered design.

After filing for your registered design, the IPO aim to get back to you within 1 month. If all is ok you will receive confirmation and a registered design certificate. The certificate contains a registered design number. It is common practice to refer to your registered design number on your product packaging to deter potential copy cats. If for any reason there is a problem with registering your design, the IPO will get back with their objections. You will have 2 months to respond to this or your application will be terminated. There is an appeals process should you not be happy with the response.

You can file your designs in other countries. Other countries have slightly different design protection systems. Most countries will except your UK registered design filing date on the condition that you file for design protection within 6 months of this date. There is also an EU system called registered community designs that cover the whole of the EU. As I am writing this book the UK has just voted to leave the EU, so I assume this will no longer be an option for British people in the future.

DESIGN RIGHT

Design right is the automatic protection that you have over your designs. In theory, this protects your design for 10 years from when it is first sold, or 15 years from when it was first created, whichever expires first. The design right does not protect patterns but does protect the shape and configuration.

Although design right is automatic, you will need to prove it is your design. To do this you can store information regarding your design with a bank or solicitor, or you can send yourself this information via registered, dated post and keep it unopened.

A registered design is more of a tangible asset than a design right and therefore would offers you a more formalised official protection. It is a much more simple process to licence out or sell a registered design as it can be transferred over in a formal process. This gives you more options to profit from your idea. Also, a registered design is a more credible protection which potential investors take more seriously than a design right.

TRADEMARKS

Another form of intellectual property well worth considering filing for is a trademark. If you have thought of a good name for your product or business you may well be able to protect it with a trademark. A trademark will stop others naming their products with your brand name, or anything too similar. Having a registered trademark allows you to put the symbol ® on your trademarked name to deter the copycats. A trademark will add another string to your intellectual property bow which is good news if you wish to license your product or sell the idea to another company.

CRITERIA FOR TRADEMARKS

Trademarks can be made of the following;

- Words
- Sounds
- Logos
- Colours

Or a combination of the above

A trademark is not allowed to be offensive. It must not describe the product or service, i.e. if it were the name for a chocolate bar; the actual trademark must not contain the word chocolate. The trademark must not be misleading i.e. you could not describe a chocolate bar as a vegan product if it contained diary. Also it cannot be a 3-dimensional shape associated with the category of the trademarked product, i.e. a trademark for a chocolate tea pot must not have the shape of a teapot in the trademark.

Your trademark must not be too common or non-distinctive. For example it cannot be a vague statement like 'simply the best'.

A trademark must not look too similar to state symbols. So you cannot use the Union Jack image or something that looks like a hallmark.

You will need to check that your trademark is not already registered within the class you would like it to be registered in. If it already exists, or one very similar exists, in the same class category, it is likely to be rejected. To check if a trademark is already registered, go to the IPO website's trademark search feature. You can see what has already been registered in each class. There is also a guide to see what class or classes you need to register your trademark in.

If you are having difficulties in placing your product into the correct category, just ask the experts. I had difficulty with one of my products and the IPO were very helpful. A trademark examiner emailed me their opinion which I then went along with. There is an online guide to trademarks available on the IPO website that you should read prior to applying.

The standard fee of is £170 for trademark registration. This registers your trademark in one class category. If you wish to register your trademark in additional categories, this will cost you an additional £50 per category.

There is an option to only pay half the fee of £200 (£100) upfront for the examination stage. Then once your trademark is through the examination stage, you pay the remaining £100 and your trademark gets registered. I chose this option when I was not sure whether my trademark was going to pass the examination. This is a less risky option if you are not sure it will pass. It maybe that you have a straight forward case you are fairly confident will pass and paying the full fees is a better option. You will save £30 and time on the administration process.

After you apply, the IPO advise that they will assess your application and get back to you within 20 days. If all is well, they will publish your application in the trademarks journal. There is a window of 2 months in which the public get to view your application in the journal and, if they wish, oppose to your application. If anyone believes your application infringes on their own trademark, or have any other reason it should be rejected, they can raise an objection. Any objections have to be resolved prior to your trademark being registered. You will have to resolve any objection by negotiating with the opposing party or legally challenge them. This may cost you money in legal fees. Hopefully your application will not be opposed, or if it is you can find another way round this without getting legal help. This may be by negotiations or just change your trademark so everyone is happy.

If you wish to protect your trademark internationally, there is a system in place called the Madrid Protocol which is managed by the WIPO. If you wish to take advantage of this system, you need to take action within 6 months of filing your UK trademark to retain the same UK priority date.

COPYRIGHT

Copyrights protect art and literature works. Copyright protection is automatic so you do not have to do anything. You should be aware of what it protects in order to take full advantage of it. See the below list detailing the scope that copyrights can cover;

- Any written work
- Computer programmes
- Illustrations, free hand or computer generated
- Sculptures
- Architecture
- Songs

- Plays
- Videos, films, TV programmes

This may include any literature associated with your invention. So your invention can be protected by a patent, and the label, instructions and any literature by copyright.

You do not need to do anything to protect your work with copyright law. Copyright protection is automatic. You can express this protection on your copyrighted material with the © symbol. It is common practice for people to put some sort of copyright statement on any material they do not wish to be copied. For instance there is often a statement at the start of a book that could typically read 'all material the ownership of (name) © copyright 2016'. You can state this copyright statement on any labelling/ marketing/ literature that you associate with your product. Using a copyright statement does not actually change your level of legal protection, but it can deter other from attempting to copy your material.

Copyright is a little less straight forward form of protection than the other forms, as there is no formal registration. This means that a copyright infringement may be a little tricky to prove. There are ways of making this a little easier for certain items. For instance, musicians can add protection to their artistic material by posting copies of new music recordings to themselves. Recorded post must be used to allow the date it was sent to be captured.

As with other forms of intellectual property protection it is not just about the filing and knowledge of copyrights, it is about having the legal back up should something go wrong. If you have your idea copied, you will need to take the appropriate legal action in order to get any sort of compensation. Hopefully, if it has got to the point of someone copying your idea, it will mean that you have an excellent idea, and you are already profiting from it. If this is the case then it may be that you can afford the legal help required. It would be more of a shame not to give your product a chance in the market in the first place due to fears over copycats than actually having your idea copied once you have had a go at producing it.

Chapter 14 The Final stages

Substantive examination

The final stage of your UK patent application is the substantive examination. You have to apply for the substantive examination within 6 months of your patent publication. This should usually be around 18 months after you initial UK filing date. You must file for the substantive examination within the time limit or your application will be considered withdrawn. Once filed, your application will be examined further. The examiner will take into account the initial IPO search report and any objections received as a result of your patent publication. They will be looking for any reasons why your application does not meet the requirements as set out by patent law. The substantive examination will cost you £100 if filed by post or £80 online.

At this point that the IPO are likely to send you correspondence requesting your response to some questions. They may question a few aspects of your application and expect you to compromise on the scope of some of your claims. Sometimes they ask you to change your claims slightly. This is to narrow down the scope of technology that your patent covers. As an independent inventor, the IPO give you a lot of advice. So at this stage it is advised to talk through the results of your substantive examination with your examiner. They are likely to be very reasonable with you and advise you exactly what to do in terms of any changes required to your patent claims. And then that is it. All being well your patent will be granted and you can crack open the champagne. Just bear in mind that this can be a very long process.

You patent application can be accelerated by filing for the substantive examination at the same time as your request for a search. This can speed things up by up to 18 months. However, the risk with this is you have to pay for the search and substantive examination before you have obtained the examiner's search report. The IPO search report may suggest to you that your idea will not receive a granted patent and you would have wasted money paying for the substantive examination. Also at the search report stage you may wish to withdraw and change your application without filing for a substantive examination. So accelerating your application in this way is only recommended if you are confident your idea is original and if you are afraid someone else is developing a similar idea at the same time as you.

INTERNATIONAL FILING

Once you have your UK patent application filed, you may wish to start thinking about international applications. International filing does start to get slightly more complicated and rather expensive. You have to start taking action for international applications within one year of your original UK filing date. This enables you to use your this date as your international priority date. This means other countries that you file for protection in will recognise this as the date you invented your idea. So you will have to consider the international options within 1 year of filing your UK patent.

There are a few choices when it comes to international protection. You can apply directly to each country or you can use what is known as a PCT application. PCT or Patents Corporation Treaty is a way of securing a world-wide priority filing date in one application. It reserves your right to file your patent worldwide for around 18 months. During these 18 months you must file patent applications for each country that you sort after patent protection. After 18 months, you lose your right to file your patent internationally with your original filing date. If you do not take the PCT route, you will have to file for patents in each country you wish to have protection within 1 year of your UK filing date. This 1 year may differ slightly for different countries. So basically the PCT option buys you extra time to consider your international options.

PCT ROUTE

As with the UK patent filing, the general advice you will see with respect to PCT and international patent applications, is to seek professional advice. I believe the PCT application process is almost purely an administrative process which is presented to seem a lot more complicated than it is, or needs to be. The advice and guidance provided by the PCT is not particularly helpful. It makes it all seem overly complex and it really is not. The costs however are relatively high in comparison to the UK filing fees. At the time of print a complete PCT application will cost you £2558. This is broken down into a few different fees. I would strongly recommend that you only proceed with this if you are confident that your product is making you enough money to justify this cost or you have reasonably certainly that you will benefit enough to justify the cost. So you have 1 year after filing your UK patent to really get things underway and make the decision of whether or not the international fees are justified.

PCT INTERNATIONAL STAGE

The PCT route is split into two different stages. The first stage is known as the international stage. This is where you file your original application within 1 year of your original UK filing date. You have to send in copies of your original UK patent application along with several forms. The result of this is that you have your original UK filing date reserved within the countries covered by the PCT. These countries include all developed nations where you could profit from your idea. You have your original UK priority date reserved for 18 months after the PCT application is filed. During this time the PCT will conduct a search in addition to the UK IPO search already taken place. Also the PCT will publish your application, so your patent will be searchable world-wide.

Around 6 months after filing your PCT application, you will receive their search report. This is similar to the UK IPO search report. It will highlight any reason they see for not granting your patents worldwide. As per the UK IPO search results, this will include copies of any cited prior art. This search report is the PCT's opinion and will not actually stop your international patent applications. However, the results of the PCT search will be forwarded to any country where you proceed with your patent applications and also to the UK IPO. This means the results can be used as evidence by any country for refusing to grant you a patent. You have a small time frame in which to respond to the PCT search results with any changes you wish to make to your claims and any objections you may have to the points raised.

PCT NATIONAL STAGE

Around 18 months after you file your international PCT form, you have to make a decision on whether to file nation applications. You will need to decide what countries you require protection in. For each country that you wish to have protection in, you need to file individual applications. Each country has their-own system. Even though most of these are fairly similar; they will have slightly different rules. You may require you application to be translated for some applications in foreign speaking countries.

By this stage, you should hopefully know exactly where you require protection and whether it is worth your while. Hopefully you know your idea is very profitable and you can afford professional help to file patents where you need to. Costs for filing patents in individual countries may not be excessive in comparison with the UK but these will stack-up if you want protection in several countries. You will have to carefully consider the benefits of protection in each country.

FINAL THOUGHTS

Hopefully you have found this guide informative and inspiring. There is no reason not to give your idea a chance, no matter what it is. You should now know how to take the first steps in protecting your idea and hopefully have the confidence to progress things further. You now do not have worry about intellectual property protection, just go for it. Remember that if and when the big money starts rolling in, this is your cue to get the professionals to step in and take over, advising you on how to take things further in the best way. Don't let the big fees put you off, get the ball rolling now yourself. There is no reason you cannot do this and now you have knowledge of the systems, take advantage of them. Best of luck.

If you have any friends that you believe could benefit from the information in this book, please recommend it to them. We all know someone who is constantly suggesting ideas for products. Let these friends know they can take their ideas somewhere with the information shared in this book. They may well be very grateful. Please get in touch with me with any further questions, feedback and let me know how you get along using this book. I will endeavour to get back to anyone who takes the time to send me an email. To get in touch please visit the website for this book,

www.fileaukpatent.co.uk,

or email neil@fileaukpatent.co.uk

Printed in Poland
by Amazon Fulfillment
Poland Sp. z o.o., Wrocław